Being Centered

Positively Contagious!

By Roman Oleh Yaworsky

Published and distributed by Spirit Unleashed™
www.spiritunleashed.com
Miami

Printed in United States of America
by AC Graphics, Inc.
www.acgraphics.com

ISBN 13: 978-0-9794040-09

ISBN 10: 0-9794040-0-2

Acknowledgements

Sharing their light

This book draws on my personal experiences. Many people have left their impressions with me. Through being with them, I have learned much and therefore, I honor and thank them all.

A number of people have shared their light in ways that are particularly meaningful to the writing of this book, and I would like to take the opportunity to express my debt to them.

I express my gratitude to my spiritual teachers, among them, the Karmapa, Swami Muktananda and Swami Chidvilasananda. Without their Grace, little would have been realized.

For being who she is and pointing me in the right directions, I express my thanks and debt to my wife Susana Sorí who took on the task of supervising the editing. Without her support, encouragement and sharing of her light and intellect, this book would never have begun. Some of the insights and directions came out of direct collaboration between us.

My thanks to Judith Kaiser, Sonja Mitchell, Tobey Milne and Rick Schwartz for reading over some of my earlier manuscripts and giving me the comments and feedback that helped this book and myself to grow. I am also indebted to them for their suggestions towards the editing of this book.

For their support and warm hearts, I thank both Olga Kostur and Olga Sorí, my two mothers.

I would like to thank Jona Cerwinske for helping to suggest the title for this book and Gus Casamayor for his encouragement and help in getting this book printed.

Finally, I would like to thank you, the reader, for reaching out towards this book. May you find what is needed to take you forward.

Roman Oleh Yaworsky

Contents

Appendix

Prologue

There are two directions for healing. One direction asserts the need for individuals to learn to adapt or to become whole within the framework of their society. The other, establishes the need for the individuals to find their unique self before re-entering the society. In many ways the former is the standard of modern cultures, the latter of more primitive or indigenous cultures.

Modern culture has for the most part condemned the primitive or indigenous, but people need to be warned that they will eventually die alone, that life is both an individual experience and ultimately a primal, if not intrinsically primitive situation, that has been altered by culture. The path of adaptation is artificial; the path of re-connection is vital and very real. Often the choice is made, as with most things in life, on the basis of fear and ignorance of one's true nature, and a life lived from fear has really not been lived at all.

For individuals who seek to be free, to act out of their core and out of their true nature, the experience of many of the modern processes for healing the soul have often been very disappointing. Instead of help in freeing themselves of the entanglements from which they may seek refuge, more often than not, they may find themselves processed and entangled in the beliefs of their counselors. In a sense people come to escape the game that they have been caught in, and instead of freedom, they end up being asked to adapt to the counselor's game.

Why does this happen? Why is the inner journey ignored? Part of the answer lies in the widespread belief that children start out wild, and need to be socialized in order to become true human beings. Otherwise, they are a wolf-child, a wild child, and therefore a burden to society. There is also the sense of the child as being born in sin or ignorance, and that they need to be saved, taught, disciplined, redeemed or broken in, in order to fully function.

What is often disregarded is that children are reaching out from their own unique spirit and heart in expressing love and seeking to share and to belong. We are amazed by the incredible pace at which infants progress towards their own understanding, and towards communicating and affecting their world.

At some stage, often as soon as we can, we take it upon ourselves to affect the progress of infants and leave our own mark on it. At first it is simple, like getting their attention and response or getting them to utter the sounds and words that we want to hear. Later, it becomes more complex and intimidating, as we insist that they perceive the world the way we want them to, and we are willing to punish them when they assert their own ways of being.

For the most part, the education that children get, either from their parents or from the society through their parents, peers and teachers, is about adapting rather than encouraging. It is about wrapping them in the swaddling clothes that makes them manageable, controllable and vessels in which to fill the continuance of the culture. The sense of the individual with his or her own rights and needs is a very modern phenomenon, and so as a culture we may accept this more enlightened concept, but for the most part we continue with the old ways of bringing children up, as we were brought up. That way does not encourage a child to be centered.

In order to break this spell, we need to wake up to our experience of life through our hearts, soul and spirit. This book is a journey towards that heart. It is a journey I have taken and it is a journey that I now share. It is a journey towards being centered.

Introduction

Why I wrote this book

The material in this book is intended to help people cross through their challenges and times of transition. For this reason, I have tried to keep things simple. Many of the concepts and ideas are original. Therefore the material of this book may give the reader a different interpretation of the dynamics of growth than is commonly held.

This book started as a set of notes and suggestions that I gave to my clients over the years. I found myself creating these suggestions, partly because I could not find this material anywhere else, and partly because much of what I found, I could not offer easily to my clients. Although there are great texts available that cover phenomenal areas of knowledge and understanding, the time and preparation necessary to make beneficial use of these resources takes more effort or devotion than most clients can offer during their personal times of crisis.

In our culture I find many important concepts that define who we are, how we function and how we heal are distorted or ignored. Often, situations that are unhealthy are considered normal, and many of the available structures and support systems seem to be focused on helping us function in society, but do not address living our lives for optimal fullness and potential.

I have taken the premise that being more fully alive and centered not only improves our ability to function in any situation, but also helps to release the hold of our past issues by shifting towards being in the moment and in our hearts. I maintain that the processes and techniques to help us move forward and towards integrity with our selves and our feelings are fairly simple and straightforward to apply in our lives.

This book is intended to shed some light on how we interact, both inwardly and outwardly, how we tend to get stuck, and to offer some suggestions and means to help us return to our true nature, to who we really are. We really are meant to be in joy and in our hearts. We really are meant to share that joy and heart with others, and when we are free to do so, that joy is contagious!

This book was designed to be read in sequence. However, I have reintroduced some of the background in each chapter so that the reader has the choice of pursuing sections in the order of their interest. A glossary has been included near the end of the book, to help clarify the meanings of the terms and concepts that are being used throughout this book.

Roman Oleh Yaworsky

Part 1
The Foundation

Being Centered: Positively Contagious!

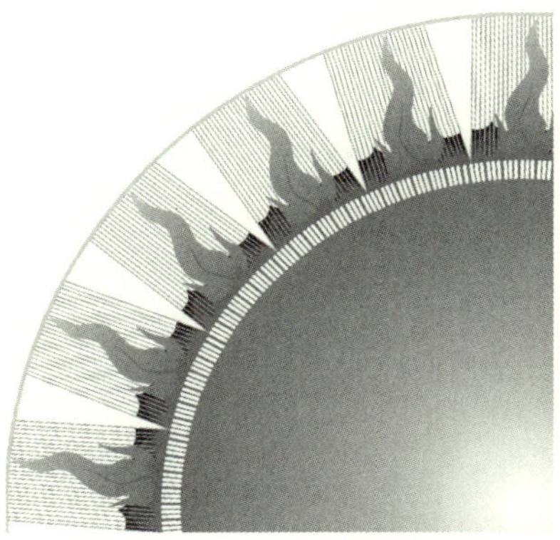

Why is Being Centered Positively Contagious?

There are two choices in life:

You can choose to be positively contagious – you can live your own life, your own dreams through being centered in who you are and experience the joy, courage and freedom revealed in your heart.

When you are centered, when you are in your heart, you are alive! Not only are you alive, but you inspire others to be alive. Aliveness is contagious. It is what everyone seeks, even if they don't know it. The aliveness that comes from being fully in the moment, fully in your own joy is priceless. Yet in its immediacy it is always present. We search for it in the things around us, but it is present when we find ourselves. It is only a heartbeat away.

Or, you can choose to live disconnected from your center and become a negative influence and drain on others. It is a choice of living and working for the dreams and hearts of others, all the while, believing the lie you may have created that others are responsible for what you have done and what you feel.

All the other choices are nothing more than variations of these two choices. Ultimately you have to choose whether you are going to live this life for you or whether others are going to live your life for their own benefit. It is your choice and your responsibility. The thing is, everything that you do that is not from your heart is ultimately an illusion. And the price of that illusion is a wasted life.

I trust, dear reader, that you are willing to risk being more fully alive and aware. Take this book to heart. It is said that in order to learn you have to be open to making mistakes. In this manner, at least, I admit to having learned much. And so I offer the fruits of that process.

In part one of this book, we will be looking at how we became separated from our center and our hearts and as a result we became separated from the immediacy of our feelings.

It is difficult to regain our core and our center through intellect, will and intention alone. This book is really about a short cut. That short cut is through the heart. When we return to our connection with our own heart, it takes us closer to our core, and we become centered. Then our courage and joy shine to others. This process is contagious. As you open up to your own joy, your own joy will teach you how to open up even more. As you own your own power, your own power will teach you how to open up to more. As this process spreads through you, others will seek you out that they may also open their hearts. They will seek your encouragement and example. It is positively contagious!

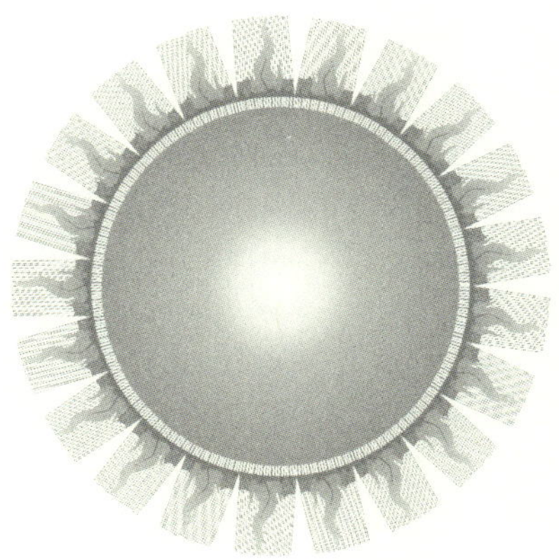

Being Centered

Living from your authentic self

To Thine Own Self Be True

William Shakespeare

What is being Centered?

There is a fundamental principle that governs how we live our lives and experience the world around us. That principle is our connection to our core, our sense of who we truly are, on the inside. Our connection to our own core, our ability to be in the moment, to be in our feelings and in our hearts, is where our power, joy and enthusiasm come from. When we have this connection, we are centered. Each of us has experienced that connection to our own core. We crave it. It makes life worthwhile.

Playing the drum

Playing the drum is one way that I have experienced a connection to my core. I remember when I first started learning to play the drum, it was a new experience and I practiced for hours and days on end, pushing myself to learn all of the rhythms and to get it right. When I began to play in a group, in front of people, I would start out so seriously, with such a sense of responsibility. I was careful not to make mistakes, and so I concentrated on being a good musician. Unfortunately, I was trying to play the drum from my fear. I felt like someone holding on tightly to the reigns of wild horses, afraid to let go. It was my own fear that I was about to make a mistake, that stalked me and held me back.

Then, after a while, I took a risk. I relaxed. I let go. I stopped playing from my fear, and I began to play from my heart. The things with which I had learned to hold myself back, vanished. In their place was the spontaneity of the moment. My fingers would play rifts and rhythms I had not even heard before. The playing flowed. It took me deeper into the moment.

Taking the risk of playing from my heart, of choosing the courage of being in the moment, also had an effect on others and soon a feeling of immediacy and power would fill the room. Time changed. I was no longer playing the drum, my heart was playing. Not just my heart; I could feel every other heart in that room. The playing was effortless, transformative and full of joy and heart.

It is to re-experience this state, to be fully centered and immersed in my heart, and to share that passion with others that I love to drum.

The magic of being centered

There is magic when we play or act from our heart. It doesn't even matter so much how much skill is being expressed. What matters is that connection that we make within ourselves. That is what the audience comes to feel. People are drawn to experience the transformative power of a performance that arises from the heart of a musician or actor. This is what we are willing to line up for and pay money to experience. We seek that connection and courage in others to help us reconnect to our own center, heart, joy, immediacy and power.

There is magic when we live from our hearts, when we experience life by being open to it and when we are able to fully receive what is offered to us. That openness, that trust, extends to the world around us and also to ourselves.

The magic of that trust in the world is that it invites grace and luck. It helps to align us with the experiences that we need, and it helps us to recognize what we need when it comes along in our lives.

The magic of that trust in ourselves invites faith in our own spirit, in our own core. It helps to align us with the experiences that we need on the inside; the answers, revelations and visions that help us live greater lives. It helps us to reconnect to the 'universal heart,' to that sense of deep connection with the world around us. That magic is positively contagious.

Why is being centered important in today's world?

Being centered saves you from giving your life away.

Centering is vital. There is no choice in being alive other than to be centered in something. The ideal center is you. In this book I will stress that the heart is the means to regain that center.

When you are not in that ideal center, when you are off-balance, when you are not in your heart, the need to center pulls you to center in things and people that do not connected you to your core, that do not connect you to your heart.

Bob Dylan wrote a song entitled *Gotta Serve Somebody*.[1] Some of you may be familiar with it. The song says that you may be this or have this or that, but that ultimately you still have to 'serve somebody!'

One way of interpreting what the song said is that no matter whom or what you identify with being, you serve what you center on. Where you center can take you to your highest, or it can bring you down. It is your choice what you center on, but you can't escape the fact that you have to center on something. And that is what you serve, that is what you place your energy behind, and that then determines your fate.

Therefore, center on your own highest good, and to get there, start with your own heart.

Centeredness is not selfishness

People often confuse being centered with being selfish.

Being centered, means taking care of ourselves and being responsible for our own happiness. Who else is going to be responsible? Being centered is about being honest and real. It is about being real with ourselves and with others. It is about being real with our feelings and with what we want.

Selfishness is about trying to fill a void. It is about trying to fill a need by not taking into account the honoring of others, nor the honoring of oneself. It is about putting the need ahead of the heart. It happens when you're not in your heart. It happens when you are not honest or real with yourself because you are disconnected from your heart.

When you are centered, you are in your heart, you do not identify yourself with a void, and so there's nothing to fill.

Often children get confused over selfishness when their intentions are misunderstood or misrepresented by their parents. This can occur when a child asks for a toy and instead of the parents saying "*We don't have enough money for that*" they say "*You are being selfish.*" Now the child has come to understand that if they ask for what they want, they are being selfish. This is very unfortunate. We need to clear this misunderstanding, so that we can act for own best interest. We must be centered, so that we can be in our hearts, in our true feelings, and open to being in the moment and to the experience of joy.

A culture of being off-center

To an ever-increasing extent, we experience being pulled away from our center in today's modern world. We are at risk of being bombarded by so much information and noise in the form of advertising and bias from publications, television, the internet and other media.

We are told that we will be happy if we buy this soft drink, that we will be sexy if look a certain way, if we buy this car or use this deodorant. We are told that we are suffering because we are not taking this drug. Advertising is not only information; it is also often designed to mold us, to turn us into consumers, and in that process, to pull us away from what we wanted and towards what others want. Often the advertising is designed to pull us off center.

What we learn to believe about ourselves from our culture

Ironically, our own culture praises success, but underscores failure. We are rarely told in television commercials that we have enough, or that who we are is fine. Instead, we are told that we lack this to be happy, or if we get that, we will avoid embarrassment. We are willing to work long hours for a chance of joy in two week stints once a year. We are asked to postpone joy, until we can afford it, until we get married, have children, get an education, or retire.

We have to be very careful not to become a victim of being molded and pulled away from being centered. The path to being centered does not come through watching more television, by buying more products, or by trading what we want or who we are for something that might be in the future. We do not live in the future and although some of us try, we do not live in the past either. We live in the present. We live through our hearts and in being centered. This we have to protect. Otherwise our experience of living is diminished.

The advantage of pulling people out of their center

Why would anyone want to pull anybody else out of his or her center? It is the way most people argue, fight, confront or engage in most conflicts. It is what works most of the time!

Pulling someone out of their center is a classic way of defeating an opponent in martial arts or in a business confrontation. If you have ever watched two people grappling each other in a judo contest, you will see them trying to knock each other off balance while seeking to maintain their own. Each competitor will repeatedly try a move to throw his adversary when he senses that there is an opening, that the other is caught off guard. It is only when the opponent is actually out of his center, through losing his concentration, focus or balance, that the throw is successful.

High stakes business negotiations can be the same way. Each 'opponent' tries to show their own strengths while at the same time taking advantage of the weaknesses of the other. This is why the three-piece blue business suit or wearing black is important! It is a show of strength.

We tend to encounter many of these strategies of knocking the other off balance among kids. Children apply leverage through name calling, threats of exclusion from the group and by making fun of the other. In a sense this is done to establish who is important and who is off balance. The winner of this conflict becomes the leader of his pack. The loser's defeat through loss of their center and connection to their core becomes a demonstration of the leader's power.

Being centered is the best defense. The degree to which children are successful with their friends and peers has a lot to do with how centered they are, how they have been encouraged to be themselves and how they have resisted losing center and adapting to the wishes and needs of others. The enormous need that children have to fit in with peers and friends, challenges their inner strength and faith in themselves. How successful children become in retaining their center and faith in themselves has great bearing on their future choices and success in the world.

What happens when we are not centered?

When we are not centered, when we are not aligned with our nature and we do not experience that connection in our hearts, we also do not experience connection with the hearts of others. We move out of alignment with our friends, family, the people we interact with, and with the rest of the universe.

The consequences of this disconnection, are that we attract experiences that tell us the universe does not support who we are. When we are confronted with this lack of support, rather than addressing the dis-connection to our own hearts, we tend to act as if our feelings are a consequence of the actions of other people. In this way we begin to center on them and what they want in order to gain their support or we may blame them as the cause of our pain and disconnection.

Either way, our stance automatically makes others more important to us than we are to ourselves. We place ourselves in a reactive posture to the power of other people to affect us. As a result, not only do we give away some of our personal power, we also give away some of our sense of aliveness in the process. We make others responsible for our own hearts!

This is what happens when we are not centered. When we don't center in our own being, and in our own hearts, we are pulled to being centered to the needs and actions of others.

The 10 Hints that you have lost your center

Here are 10 hints that you are off balance or not centered in your interactions with others. Are any of these your pattern?

Hint 1: You seek others to be your center. When you lose connection to your own core and heart, you seek others to be your center. When you seek to lean on the people in your life instead of taking responsibility for your own healing, you leave yourself open and vulnerable to be manipulated by their needs and for them to define your worth and who you are.

Hint 2: You start to feel powerless. When you lose your center, you feel powerless. You start to feel that you cannot change your situation for the better, or to say what you feel or what you want. You begin to believe that you are not important, that you don't matter. Then it becomes okay if someone ignores your best interests, or if you do not get your needs met.

Hint 3: You try to adjust to the needs of others. You try to please them or make them like you, because in losing your center, the hearts of others become more important than your own. You then center on their approval and their acceptance of you.

Hint 4: You begin to blame other people. When your attempts at adjusting to others fail, or you make them responsible for your loss of center, you begin to blame others in your life.

Hint 5: You become irresponsible with your heart. You begin to honor others more than yourself. You may act totally responsible in your duties at work and seemingly in your dealings with others in your need to be accepted, liked or approved of. At the same time, you ignore your own best interest and feelings.

Hint 6: You begin not to take care of your feelings, your heart or your best interests. Instead your focus shifts to taking care of other things. You begin to put inconsistent value on the people and things in your life in direct proportion to their hold on you. You become more reactive and more easily ruffled and you increasingly act out of your fear.

Hint 7: You begin to be more pessimistic about the future. Your experience of losing your center is a contraction. As a result, there is less expansiveness towards the future.

Hint 8: You often ignore what happens inside of you. When your focus is on your reactions to others, you tend to ignore yourself. However, what happens inside of you is far more important.

Hint 9: You begin to lose trust in yourself as you become disconnected from your center on the inside. You often experience that separation in your heart, in your own sense of value, your sense of worth and in your own will.

Hint 10: You begin not to like yourself. Having lost your center, you begin not liking the choices you are making with your life. In time you may experience difficulty in liking yourself and whom you have chosen to become.

All of these things happen as a result of losing your center. In this way, you become contracted to your own spirit and to your own energy. These inward disconnections are primary. When you do not address them, you form emotions and negative emotional states. And then you begin to define yourself by these very disconnections.

How do you regain center?

You never lose your core. You never lose your center. You never lose your heart. What you lose is your connection. And in order to regain your center, you need to regain your connection. How do you do that? You do it by reconnecting to the place where that relationship was first lost, where that separation was first felt, and that place is in your heart.

How do you reconnect to your heart?

In order to reconnect to your heart you need to stop avoiding your heart. What do I mean by that? Well, we often edit, ignore, avoid, or try to control what comes from our hearts.

Have you ever had the experience of being asked how you feel about something, and you find yourself lying because the truth is not what someone else wants to hear? When you start down this path, you often begin to lie to yourself also. Then your own internal dishonesty begins to separate you from your true feelings.

We have to learn to stop doing that. We have to become aware of our feelings and of what our heart is trying to tell us. And we have to learn to take care of our heart. As we do these things, our connection to our heart will increase and this will pull us back to center.

The process of returning to center and the means to do it through our heart forms much of the basis of the rest of the book.

Chapter summary

In this chapter you were introduced to the importance of being centered in your life and in today's world. We looked at the consequences of not being centered. In a very real way, being centered is being alive as yourself, in your energy and in your heart. It is not selfishness. In fact, selfishness occurs when people are not centered.

In this chapter, we received 10 hints that can alert us to times when we are not centered or not taking care of our feelings.

We are often told to smile and look good in order to be liked and accepted. When you are centered, the smile is genuine and you radiate. In that stance, you are positively contagious!

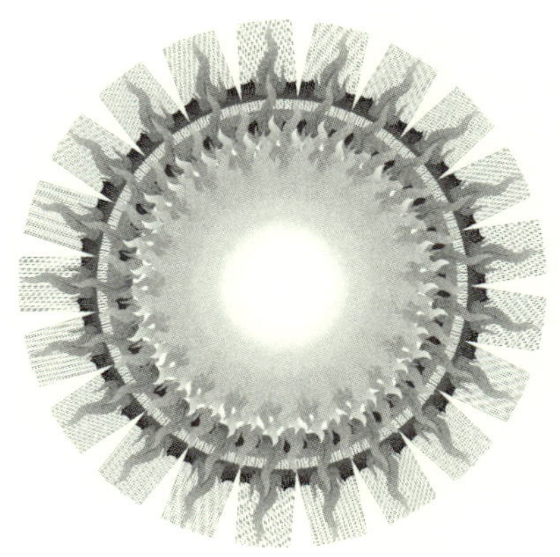

The Inner Child:
Learning to act from your core through your inner child

What is the inner child?

When we see pictures or illustrations of saints, we often see them surrounded by children or animals. Have you ever wondered why? It is not because they are good or bad, deserving or undeserving. What children and nature all have in common is their openness to receiving what is offered. Children tend to be more open to life and to experiencing the fullness of each moment. That very openness and willingness to be alive can be very captivating, as witnessed by any group of adults that are near an infant or young child.

Often, as we grow up and adapt to the world around us, that innocence, purity of being and openness seems to vanish. In reality, it is still there, but for most people, it is hiding within them. That part that for many is hiding is often referred to as 'the inner child.'

Various traditions warn us about the actions that take us out of that experience of innocence and openness that comes when we maintain that connection to our hearts and to being centered in our own joy. The results of these actions are often referred to as the 'sins,' the 'thieves,' the 'traps,' the 'bad company,' and the 'pitfalls.' Through fear, pride, or entrenched emotions and patterns, we end up seeking an outward definition of who we are. The trap is that this outer identification separates us from who we need to be, from how we need to act, to feel, to love and to be centered in our hearts.

How did you lose your inner child?

We start out in life seeking to share our innocence, joy, and enthusiasm that is our birthright with those that we come in contact with. We blossom and move forward in our own personal unfoldment when we are encouraged and when we experience that others value, appreciate and support who we are and what we offer through their actions, their expressions and their words.

For some, there are experiences that indicate that what is being offered is not encouraged or appreciated in some way. In order to receive what is sought, children tend to adapt to what appears to be expected of them. They say to themselves, *"If I become what my parents seem to want, then they will love me."* Over time, each experience of adapting takes them farther and farther away from their true nature, from their spontaneity and self-effulgent joy. They learn to trade their own love of themselves for the hopeful love of their parents. They learn not only to adapt to the expectations of their parents, but to others, to their job, to their friends, to their spouse and even to their own children. The problem is that after all of that adapting, the place inside, of innocence, joy and enthusiasm may have been ignored to such an extent, that it becomes difficult to access. At that point, recovering the inner child can take effort. The fact that there is even an issue here may go unnoticed until there is a major crisis.

The mid-life crisis

One of the common ways that the inner child is revealed later in life is during the so-called mid-life crisis that marks the early forties. This is really a crisis of the inner child needing to be taken seriously. It hits those people who have adapted to the needs of their job, to responsibilities and to getting ahead, and especially those who have ignored their true feelings.

The restlessness of these times is directly related to a conflict between an inner need to be alive and free and an outer need to be safe, successful and accepted. That conflict can sometimes result in quitting careers or relationships. For some people it can amount to a need to take a last fling at life while they are still in their prime. More often than not, the outward choices do not solve the dilemma. The solution lies in becoming more alive through becoming more aware, connected and expressive of feelings, and through assuming the responsibility of taking care of these feelings.

The mid-life crisis is an opportunity to reconnect to the part of you that is alive, joyful and willing to take the risk of living life more fully. It is an opportunity that must not be ignored. **The key to going successfully through this transition is to become aware of your feelings and what you want, and to become more aware of why you do things and for whom.** Life is a partnership of what you want out of life and what life expects of you. The mid-life crisis is a time to reconnect with what makes you alive and to fully engage your needs and joy in that partnership.

Summer holidays and sick days

There are other times in our lives that give us opportunities to make shifts and changes, away from the routines and adaptations to family, friends or work environment. Some of these times are summer holidays and sick days.

We often choose to go outside of our peer group in order to go through our personal changes and shifts in life. As children going to school, the great shifts from year to year often occur during the summer holidays. Everyone coming back has changed, grown a little physically and emotionally, and there is a return to school and to school buddies with stories about what we did during the summer. A century ago, that time may have been spent on the farm, doing chores, and helping with the harvest. Either way, it afforded a safe time to go through the necessary transitions of maturing, without the risk of peer dynamics at school.

Later, as we enter the work force, for most of us, taking off several months at a time each year is rare. Even our vacations tend to be of short duration and often scheduled with activities, plans or family responsibilities. Free time, without an agenda is difficult to manage for most people. What happens instead, are sick days.

Why people get sick in the first place is an interesting subject in its own right. My observation is that often people get sick after they relax. Sometimes work and other obligations can raise the level of stress to point where people are pushing themselves past their limit. However, even for relatively prolonged periods, most people press on, without incident. Then the task is finished, or a load of responsibility is removed. Perhaps some earned time off is taken. Surprisingly, this is when people often tend to get sick. It may seem incongruous to you that people are actually resting or recuperating when they fall to illness.

One explanation for this pattern is that people hold back on their feelings or their needs during the times that they over-push themselves. They enter a state of 'tunnel vision,' where the work they are doing, or the deadline, is more important than they are. So they put themselves on hold. All the repressed feelings and held back needs come out later, when they relax.

The degree to which people put themselves on hold can reflect how much they have done so during most of their lives. Often, it's not just recent feelings and needs, but accumulated emotions, hurts, tensions, memories and repressed issues from way back that come out. Some of these emotions may have been held for a long time and show themselves in muscle tensions, pain or even chronic illness.

Following an illness, when people re-enter their jobs and reconnect with their friends and associates, they tend to be given a grace period of a week or more, as colleagues recognize that an 'illness' has occurred and they don't expect anyone to be quite 'up to speed' for a while. That grace period gives people a chance to integrate their shifts and personal changes in relation to their jobs, co-workers and friends.

I have noticed friends who developed a much more balanced and philosophical attitude following an illness. For some, the illness was a blessing, an unplanned rest stop that rescued them from what they were doing by reconnecting them with what was important, realistic and for their benefit. In fact, the illness may have acted as a kind of emergency steam pressure release, which if not activated in time would be followed later with much more dramatic and potentially more debilitating results.

I am not advocating illness as a means to shift. I am pointing out that when people disconnect from their hearts and best interests, their own body may choose illness in order to reestablish balance. Looking at it in this way, illness can let you know that you have not been taking care of yourself, not only physically, but also at the level of spirit, feelings and joy.

Symptoms of ignoring your joy

Most people can imagine what the overly responsible expression in others looks like; the drawn out face, the wrinkles under the eyes and over the forehead, the frown, the tightness of the jaw muscles, the sad eyes, the tight lips, the contracted pupils. These are somewhat the descriptions of getting old. When you ignore your joy, when the inner child in you is kept down, you will look older and less enthusiastic. Does any of this sound familiar? What can you do to turn things around? You can begin by noticing when you hold back on your joy.

Noticing

Observe yourself when you are with other people. When people ask you how you are doing, do you shrug your shoulders and then lie? Do you tell them what you think they want to hear, or do you express yourself as you are?

When people are being playful, do you join in the fun, or do you hold yourself back? If you tend to hold yourself back, ask yourself why you do this. Is it because you are afraid of being rejected or making a fool of yourself, or is it because you have had negative experiences playing? Know that if you continue to avoid, you continue to add to the negative experiences.

Are you willing to take a small step towards being playful? Observe your state, the way you behave and the way others behave among themselves and with you. See if you can notice any patterns, habits or tendencies. Do you tend to mingle with certain people more than others? What do these people and you have in common? Notice when you hold back on your joy. Notice what happens to those that freely express this part of themselves.

Chances are that people who express their joy are more popular and successful. You have the same joy within yourself. Why not move towards expressing more of it to yourself and to others?

Connecting to your feelings

The key in learning to connect to your joy is to connect to your feelings in general. Feelings are spontaneous. When you allow your feelings to be, without editing, masking, denying or pushing them away, the experience of joy also manifests. Acceptance of your feelings, as they are, whether there is sadness or happiness, is a large step in the direction of joy and spontaneity.

The issue is that somewhere along the way, feelings may have been put on the back burner. Unless you catch yourself, you are likely to continue the process that you may have learned through adapting to the needs of others. When feelings are put on the back burner, they transform into emotions.

It is important to distinguish between feelings and emotions. People often confuse the two, but they are **very** different. Later in this book, especially in the chapter on *Feelings and Emotions* we will be looking at this distinction in greater detail. Here is an easy way to distinguish the two:

Emotions are reactive, they have a charge to them and they

hold un-integrated issues from the past. They erupt from us when our buttons are pushed, and their intensity and underlying cause has little to do with being in the present moment. They invariably take us into the past, and out of being open to what is available or being offered now.

The experience of emotions is that they take over, and we become victims of this process. Examples are rage, jealousy, discouragement, resentment, hopelessness, bitterness and guilt. Emotions take us away from being in our center and heart, and outwards towards blame and lack of trust.

The experience of feeling is more immediate. Feelings follow directly the nuances of your relationship with your heart. When you are connected to your heart, you experience feelings of connection, such as love, gladness, awe, happiness, joy and compassion. When that connection is in danger of being lost, you experience feelings of separation. These are feelings that seek immediate reconnection, such as anger, or the experience of the loss of connection, such as sadness, fear, grief, hurt, bored, tired and pain. When you acknowledge these feelings as telling you to do something to reconnect to your heart, and then you take appropriate actions, you return to feelings of connection.

Don't be too concerned if you experience initial difficulty in noticing or connecting to your feelings. If you have developed habits of editing, suppressing or ignoring your feelings, especially with others, it may take time. Know that as you work on yourself, and especially as you start taking care of your feelings, the delay you may initially experience before you know how you are feeling will shorten, until it becomes negligible. When that happens, the ability to know what you are feeling in the moment will help you in choosing appropriate actions with others.

Taking care of your feelings

After you become aware of your feelings, and have begun to accept them as they are, the next step is to take care of them. You have to become the best parent to yourself you could have ever had. You need to take care of the younger side of your nature that is intimately connected with your feelings. It is by taking care of your feelings, and quite literally demonstrating to this younger part of yourself that it is safe to feel, that the message will sink in, that it is okay to experience joy.

How does one take care of one's feelings? Let's look at an example. You are at a reception, and someone familiar to you makes an effort to approach you. They let you know how thankful they are to find a friendly and sympathetic ear. Wasting no time, they begin to tell you how awful their day was. You begin to notice your own energy is depleting. What do you do?

Do you go on listening because you identify with being a 'nice person?' Perhaps you choose to be 'polite' or 'social.' If you have a history of taking care of the problems of others before you take care of yourself, you might find yourself standing there until you are so depleted you may literally develop physical symptoms such as headache or a pain in the neck! At what point do your own feelings begin to matter? At what point do you take the action that takes care of your own feelings?

Do you make up a weak excuse so that you can leave? As you are attempting to pull away, does the other person reel you in? Is it beginning to look like you are their victim, and they are not likely to let go of their catch so easily?

Or, do you tell the person straight, and say something like *"Not today"* or *"I can't hear this today"* or *"Please talk to someone else about it - I have to go now."* You are welcome to smile, and even laugh as you say it, but be willing to put your foot down! If you are concerned with hurting their feelings, be aware that they are not concerned with hurting yours – they are after your sympathy and good energy. They are an energy thief, a vampire.

Chances are, in the example we have been using, as soon as the person realizes that you are not willing to be a victim, they will move on to better prospects. You were never responsible for their feelings. It was all an illusion. You are responsible for your own feelings. When you take on that responsibility by acting for your self and for your feelings, you add your will to the equation. When you add your own will by taking appropriate actions, you transform; you shift closer to who you were meant to be.

If you are overly concerned about hurting other people's feelings and you are willing to have your own feelings ignored and your energy drained, then alarms should be going off inside of you, and you need to take action. You are being given a choice. It is your life. Only you are responsible for your life, because you are the one that has to live it.

When people fly on a plane, there is usually a demonstration of how to use the oxygen mask. You are told to put your own mask on first before you help someone else with theirs. There is a good reason for this. Once you have your mask on, and are properly breathing, you can then help someone else, even by sharing your mask with them. If you try to help them by placing their mask on first, both of you may perish.

It is the same with feelings. If you take care of your own feelings first, then you are acting from the strength of your connection to your heart and your center. From that place, you can truly reach out to others to help them, for you have something to offer. When you do not take care of your feelings, and instead take care of the feelings of others, you are acting out of weakness and disconnection. You are letting your own heart know you are not important, and others are more important.

Caring for others and not for yourself is how we get drained and hurt around other people. When you offer yourself from this place, others do not honor you or what you give, because what is offered is suspect. You can not love someone else if you do not love yourself. You have to start with your own heart and your own feelings.

Now is the time to break an old and useless pattern. Now is the time to demonstrate to the inner child inside of you that you are going to take care of your feelings and needs, that it is safe to be alive now and in the future. That part of you has been waiting for it to be safe, all of these years, so make it so.

The 8 keys to the inner child

The inner child is about feeling and actions. It has little to do with thinking and analyzing. If you try to figure things out by ignoring your feelings then the way back will remain hidden. To uncover the way, let's look at the 8 keys that unlock the doors to our inner child:

Key 1: Your inner child speaks to you through your feelings.

In a way, your inner child is not separate from your feelings. Your inner child is the one inside of you that responds immediately to what people say and do. It hears the way a young child hears, innocently, simply and uncomplicatedly. It follows the nuances of your heart. It is the part of you that takes things literally, directly and unedited. It is the part of you that takes in life as feeling rather than thinking. It is in fact the original you, the part that breathed your first breath and experienced the world and the joy of being alive.

Key 2: Your inner child is waiting to be cared for.

Over time, the choices you have made, the actions you have taken, or that others may have taken with you or done to you, may have convinced your inner child she has not been cared for. That part of you may even still be afraid that it will never be cared for. As a result, it may no longer seem safe to feel, express or experience joy.

It is time to convince this part of you that there is someone who is more than willing and able to take care of them. It is time for you to step up, and do some convincing!

Key 3: The inner child controls how much joy you experience.

The inner child is the part of you that feels, that was there at the very beginning of your life. It is still there now. It never went away.

If you look at a tree, what you see in the trunk and main branches is what used to be the original sapling. In much the same way, your inner child is like your own trunk at the level of energy and feeling. It is the foundation to the rest of you! That part of you that feels controls how much joy you let in to your life, or how much joy you hold back to play it safe.

When you ignore this part of you, or you allow for this part of you to be rejected, then you are choosing to hold back on joy. It would be like a tree holding back on the sap running through its own trunk. It would not be good for the tree, and it is not good for you.

Take care of your trunk, and let the aliveness of the inner child flow through you fully.

Key 4: You lose your inner child when you ignore your feelings.

Your feelings are immediate. If you begin to edit them, suppress them or ignore them, then you lose connection with their immediacy. This can happen if you feel one thing, but say something else or if you become dishonest with your own feelings in your attempt to take care of the feelings of others. When you say one thing but feel something else, then you are disconnecting with this part of yourself.

Key 5: You alienate your inner child when the feelings of others matter more than your own.

You alienate your inner child when you take care of someone else but ignore yourself or your own feelings or best interests. Then you are letting yourself know, you are letting the part of you that feels directly know that it comes second, that it is less important than everyone else.

The irony, of course, is that when you are taking care of others in this way, you are really taking care of their inner child, and rejecting your own.

To give an analogy, imagine a parent being overly concerned with the welfare of someone else's children, while blatantly ignoring their own. Imagine how their children would feel, "*I don't matter,*" and the message they would receive, "*Every one else is more important.*" Unfortunately, these are the very messages that you are giving yourself, if you take care of someone else by ignoring your own welfare and feelings. People do this a lot, without realizing their patterns. They may see themselves as nice, helpful or caring. However, that caring is for others, not for themselves. Meanwhile, they suffer. An occasional acknowledgement from others will not change the fact that they have ignored their own feelings.

You are responsible for taking care of your feelings, no one else. When you do not take care of your feelings, it is you that suffers, no one else.

Key 6: When you lose your inner child you become more dependent on others.

If you act for others and ignore your own feelings and self interest, you become more and more separated from the part of you that feels joy and is alive. As a result, you become more and more dependent on others for attention and aliveness on the outside. You also risk compensating and seeking joy through addictions.

Key 7: Taking care of your feelings re-establishes trust.

When you finally begin to take care of your feelings, you give a strong and clear message to your whole system and to the part of you that feels it is finally safe to feel good, to be alive, to risk being.

The part of you that feels, the part of you that we are calling the inner child has in fact been waiting all of this time to be taken care of. It has been waiting all of this time to trust, and to be trusted. When we take care of our feelings, we act like a good parent taking care of a loved child. That is when our inner child will risk smiling and beaming. That beaming is our joy. When you take care of your feelings, you are letting yourself know it is safe to stop holding back on joy, on feeling and on being alive. That joy comes out of your heart, out of your spirit, and it is not dependent on others. It has always been there, but it needs you to take care of it. It needs to trust and be trusted.

Key 8: The greatest key is appropriate action from you.

It is important to notice feelings. We can talk about feelings. We can share them.

However, it is only through action that we demonstrate to that part of ourselves that feels deeply that it is safe to feel deeply, to risk feeling joy and to trust the rug will not be pulled out from under our feet. It is when we actually demonstrate we are taking care of our selves and our feelings while we interact with others, that we begin to trust it is alright to feel more joy. Some of those actions will be discussed in the chapters that follow.

The effects of being childlike

When you align yourself with your feelings and your heart, you will become more open to your own power and effectiveness. You will be able to risk the spontaneity of your own joy. Being playful and spontaneous is contagious. It attracts people. It is an irony that the people who try to please others by holding back on their feelings and joy, end up pushing these same people away. People do not want to be around someone that is dry or un-alive. People want to bask around open hearts and around the courage that flows from those whose hearts are opened.

Look at the way people are pulled in by infants. Their spontaneity and heartfulness is disarming. People seek to connect to them, to get their attention. Infants, although they may be at the mercy of their parents, show the courage of their feelings – they manifest their joy and their power. Look around you at the people that are successful in their dealings with others. If you look closely, you may notice that they too show the courage of their feelings, and they too manifest their power.

The effect of being childlike, is to be alive again.

A Great man is he who does not lose his childlike heart.

Mencius

Chapter summary

In this chapter, we looked at the inner child from the point of view that it was the original part of us that existed when we were born, and exists now in the immediacy of our feelings. We form a positive relationship with that inner child when we take care of our feelings and demonstrate through actions that we can trust feeling joy in the world.

We identified the 8 keys that help us understand our relationship to our inner child, how we alienate that relationship when we ignore our own best interests and how we can reestablish that relationship when we act and demonstrate we value ourselves.

In the next chapter, we will be looking at how it came to be that we disconnected from our feelings and our joy.

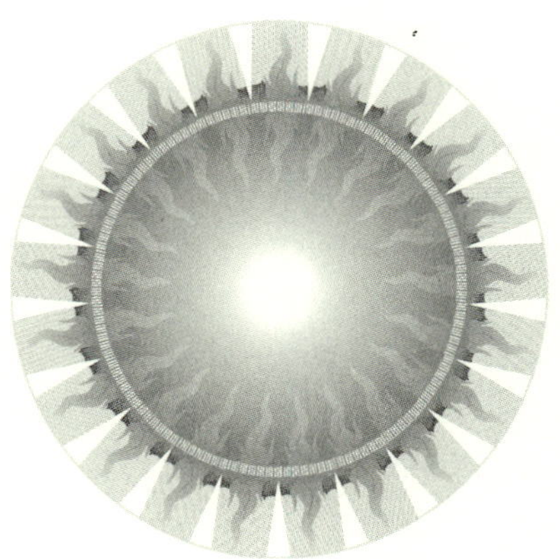

Feelings and Emotions

What underlies the ability to go from deep and profound states of connection to states bound by our emotions that separate us from our core and our hearts? How is it that we can vacillate so much and to such extremes? How is it that the same situation can result in one person laughing and another person going into rage? And why is it we tend to cling to states that are not good for us when there are better ways of being?

This chapter addresses why we shift between feelings, emotions and emotional states. This is a significant chapter that establishes how we relate to the world with our hearts. It lays the foundation for the rest of the book. I recommend that you contemplate it until it feels familiar to you.

Joy

Joy arises out of the connection to the heart and the spontaneity and freedom of being in the moment. You don't have to buy anything or be anyone else to experience joy. There are people who experience this feeling of connection regardless of the circumstances around them. These are people in all walks of life, some in good health, others not, yet, they feel joy. We are meant to feel joy. It is our home. Nevertheless, many of us wander away from our home, and become identified with not being in joy, or come to believe that joy is rare or fleeting.

Many people associate joy as something that happens to them when they get what they desire, or as a reaction to positive circumstances. This is very much the problem with joy. People are convinced that it comes from outside, that it comes from getting what you want, and that this is the process that drives the experience of joy. Because this is the cultural belief and because this is what people are conditioned to expect, joy is rarely experienced by most people. Most of the time, people do not get what they want. Surprisingly, many people, even when they do get what they purport to want, do not feel joy.

We very much live in a world where the belief is that the source of joy is somewhere outside of us, in our friends, in our partner, in our job, in money, success, reward, vacation or retirement. It is partly that we expect to find joy out there, that we have, as a culture, dug ourselves deeply into addictions and consumerism.

There is a story, attributed to the Sufis, which describes a man, on his hands and knees, searching for something near a street lamp, in the middle of the night. A policeman comes upon this scene and asks the man if he needs assistance. The man replies that he lost his keys to his house. Willing to help find them, the policeman asks the man where he remembers last seeing his keys. The man replies that he left his keys in the house. The policeman, fairly surprised, asks why the fellow is looking for them near the street lamp, when he knows that the keys are in the house! The man answers, somewhat dismayed by the question, "*Here is where the light is! I need the light in order to see!*"

It is the same with joy. We left our joy in our hearts. We locked ourselves out of our hearts through our actions, and all we have to do is return. Nevertheless, we seek joy outside, because that is where the action seems to be. That is where we were told to look. This is where the neon lights dance.

Returning to Joy

To return to joy, you simply need to re-enter your heart. You can begin to do this by noticing what you are feeling right now. Try this exercise:

If you can sit for a moment, do so. Breathe. Become aware of your breath. What are you feeling, right now? Do not try to change or act on your feelings. Simply acknowledge them. Try treating whatever comes up for you in the same way you would watch a scene on television. Just observe. Be aware of how your body feels. Try to feel the energy of your body, where it is being held, where it is moving. Do the same with any thoughts or impressions that may arise. Relax and observe. Do not try to do anything other than to continue to breathe in a relaxed manner. Let each breath act like the waves of the ocean hitting the shore, one moment foaming, the next moment receding. Let each wave of your breath take you closer to your heart. Relax your face and eyes. Allow your eyes and face to take on the gentlest form of a smile. Try closing your eyes for a minute as you continue sitting.

Now, see if you can remember a time which stands out for you as joyful and happy; a time when you allowed yourself to fully feel good. Perhaps it was meeting someone you had not seen for a long time, or seeing a beautiful sunset, or hearing a note in a song. Take the time you need for the remembrance to reveal itself. Be patient and welcoming. Search your heart. Close your eyes for a minute.

What memory came up for you? Can you taste that feeling? Do you remember the scents, the colors? How does your heart feel? Do you feel closer to your joy? Did you notice a shift in your state, even if it was slight? You may find this simple exercise is worth doing regularly, to reconnect you to your heart and joy.

This exercise demonstrates a fundamental principle of returning to joy. In order to return to your heart, in order to experience joy, all you have to do is return to an experience of joy that did connect you. Joy is not something that is manufactured. Joy is always present. **What it takes to experience joy, is to suspend the ways that you use to avoid it.**

In a way, joy is much like sleep. Sleep is rejuvenating and necessary. Some people struggle with it and even take pills regularly to fall asleep. Others just fall asleep. It is all about the willingness to let go. Joy is like that. It is about the willingness to let go of all of the things that keep us away from being in joy. After that, joy takes over.

Fear

We often take fear for granted. Infants often have a natural aversion of heights. We fear getting hurt or being embarrassed. We may naturally assume that fear is normal and that people who do not have a fear, lack something. It may surprise you to know there are people who do not experience fear as we know it, yet they lack nothing. The reason is fear is not a primary feeling. It is not something that is a given. It is a response to a loss. It is not a feeling of connection, but of disconnection. When we are connected to our hearts, our common fears evaporate.

The source of fear is in separation. The infant who shows fear of heights and of falling is avoiding being separated from secure ground. That secure ground that we all start with, is our own connection to our hearts.

When we experience a shock to our system, to our sense of who we are, that secure ground disappears for us. We experience a fall from being centered and in our hearts. We experience a drop in energy. It is the loss of connection with our core, or our heart, that results in the immediate experience of fear.

We also experience fear when we anticipate or experience the loss of something that we identify with. It is a common phenomenon to rejoice at receiving something that we value, and then to experience fear that someone may take it away from us.

There is the story of a hunter who lived in a forest. He roamed the woods freely and without fear. One day he found a barbecue stove that a camper had left behind. In the years that passed, the hunter began to use the stove daily, and he became very protective of it. Now, when he heard the leaves rustle, it was not game that came to mind for him, but fear that someone might come to steal the stove from him. Therefore, he was constantly vigilant and related his own welfare to protecting his stove. He once lived in freedom and slept under the stars. Now, he lived in fear and slept beside his stove.

When you identify with something on the outside, it often happens because you have lost some of your connection on the inside. It is the decreased flow of your inner sense of joy and connection to your heart and spirit that manifests as your outward experience of fear. The hunter lost his heartfelt feeling of freedom in the woods and replaced it with his concern for the stove. Yet, the real source of his fear was that he lost some of his inner freedom and courage, and as a result, clung to the stove much more.

Overcoming Fear through Courage

Courage comes from the heart. We often associate courage with soldiers, athletes, heroes or individuals who overcome great obstacles. What brings these people together is their demonstration of heartfulness. What sets them apart as a group is that their 'hearts' are greater than the obstacles they overcome.

You can often see a demonstration of heartfulness when you watch a team of athletes playing sports. A competing team acts out of the courage of the moment, which is determined by their heart and spirit. Spectators encourage their team and cheerleaders encourage the spectators. Watching the progress of a game can be like watching the energy of each team rising and falling, making an advance, responding or falling back. The team that wins is more often than not, the team with more heart in the moment. The losing team has less. The equation is: increase heart, increase courage; decrease heart, decrease courage.

We assume that courage is about overcoming fear, yet it is when we reconnect to our heart or core that we lose our fear. It is in reconnecting to our spirit, faith and trust that we find ourselves singing hymns or seeking prayer in times of great distress. The courage that we seek comes from that reconnection.

Courage comes from the pure freedom in the midst of the heart. Feelings and delight exist, in the moment, within that freedom. That freedom cannot be removed. What can be removed is the connection to that freedom and courage. We looked at the ways that disconnection manifests as fear in the previous section. Now let's look at how we can reconnect through courage.

The act of courage is two fold:

1. Demonstrating your trust in yourself through actions.

We need to show or prove that our own connection to our core or to our heart is more important than whatever initiated our experience of separation. This is why people go back to the place or situation that initiated their fear, and why they choose to 'go through it.' It is a demonstration of trust in themselves. That demonstration of trust validates their connection to their heart, and in doing so, reconnects them to the courage of their heart.

The key to this process is the taking back of your own power. You give away your power when you make something or someone more important than your heart. You continue to give away your power as you make others responsible for your own loss of power through blame, envy or criticism. Taking back your power requires demonstrating that you own your power and that you are responsible for it; that you trust yourself and your joy. That demonstration may be as simple as telling someone what you really feel, or in making an alternative choice in the direction of who you are or what you want. It means that you choose to strengthen your ability to feel more competent or more powerful the next time. For example, many people are afraid of public speaking and join clubs or workshops to become comfortable with being in their hearts when they speak in public.

2. Reconnecting with your core, through your heart.

Often, when we are hurt or when we are in fear, we seek

the things and people in our lives that help to reconnect us to our center and joy. This can come through spiritual practices, listening to music, going out in nature, friendships or taking time to play.

Whatever means this reconnection takes, it strengthens our trust in ourselves, in feeling and being in our heart. In doing so, we are stronger to act out of our own courage.

We can be helped in this process through encouragement from those around us. En-courage-ment is really about strengthening our own inner heart connection so that we can act from that place more freely and strongly in the world. This is why encouragement is so important for children to receive from their parents. It strengthens their connection to their hearts, and helps to support their courage and trust in themselves.

You can also encourage yourself. Often, if you examine your internal dialogue, you may find that you are telling yourself discouraging and often erroneous statements that you have acquired over time. You can just as easily replace this internal dialogue with positive and encouraging statements that pull you back to your trust in yourself.

Anger

We experience fear when there is a sense of separation or disconnection from the heart. Fear tends to immobilize us. Anger, on the other hand, holds our ability to do something about our disconnection.

There are actually two kinds of anger. The anger that arises spontaneously in response to experiencing separation from the heart, is our own 'will' trying to re-connect and reestablish its homeostasis. For example, someone is insulting us or not respecting our space. We act to address or challenge the situation before we lose more energy. The secret to this kind of anger, is that it carries our will in its immediacy. Because our will is there, we can respond in a way that re-connects us to our hearts, and deal with a disrupting situation. We can overcome our fear through action, intent or choice. **This kind of anger is a feeling that seeks**

to reconnect us to the heart.

The other kind of anger does not carry our will in its immediacy. It is emotional baggage that we still carry. Expressing this kind of anger is often fruitless and more often damaging. Because this kind of anger is an emotional response divorced of taking responsibility, there is a lack of limits or even appropriateness. This anger is rooted in blame, in making others responsible. This is the kind of anger that can be abusive, ranting, vengeful, full of rage or heartless.

I remember my martial arts instructor stressed many times that it was vital not to allow yourself to get caught in a situation which released this kind of anger. According to him, it would take days to recover the lost and wasted energy that this kind of anger consumed.

Although this anger does not carry our immediate will, it does point to the place that seeks healing, and to the place that we originally gave our will away. **This kind of anger is an emotion and it carries our wound of separation from our heart.**

Overcoming anger through will

The anger that is our feeling of disconnection often does not last long. It seeks to act so that we can become whole or to remove the obstacles or source of our experience of disconnection. There are times when anger is appropriate, because it calls us to action or asserts our worth.

Emotional anger on the other hand is rarely appropriate and can last. As mentioned earlier, emotional anger does not hold our will. Instead, it holds the giving away of our will. This is why in confrontations, people try to get their opponents angry in an emotional and reactive way. The anger acts as a wedge, disconnecting the opponents from their own will and from being centered and fully present to the situation. The anger releases the charge of past wounds, frustrations and hurts. These are the buttons that are pushed. This anger weakens people by wasting their energy, will and focus.

Engaging your emotional anger, expressing it or trying to

release the charge it holds does not work. This will only bring back the experiences of disconnection from will, hurt and blame that the anger holds. That is its nature.

On the other hand, 'bottling up' or denying your anger does not work well. **Denying your anger will only strengthen it, because in denial, you are pushing your will away all over again.**

What is the solution? You must return to your nature. You must return to the connection of your own heart. You may have to forgive yourself for holding anger, as that helps you re-connect to your heart. Forgiveness is the way to re-welcome the disowned will, which had become anger, back to the heart.

For truly overcoming anger, you have to strengthen your will and put it to work. All of the emotional anger that you hold are experiences of the frustration of your will. Therefore it is your will that you need to heal.

You heal your will every time you stand up for your heart, for your feelings, for your connection to your core and your center. **You heal your will every time you ask for what you want or need, every time you take care of your own feelings before you take care of the feelings of others.**

You strengthen your will every time you choose those actions that maintain your integrity, every time you build trust in yourself. In a way, will is always there, but you can get into the habit of not owning it, or giving it away, by making others responsible for your life. When you own your will, you strengthen your connection to your core and to your integrity. Then, there is no place for anger to develop.

How do feelings become emotions?

We have looked at joy, fear and anger. We know that feelings are closer to who we really are than emotions. The question is, why do we accumulate emotions when they are not good for us? How do feelings become emotions? And why do people confuse the two?

Part of the confusion with feelings and emotions, is that we do feel both. We experience our feelings and we experience our emotions with the same equipment. So for many of us, these tend to feel the 'same.' The difference between feelings and emotions is where that experience takes us.

We have already looked at how feelings arise from our connection with our hearts. When we are in harmony with the world, we tend to feel joy, curiosity, awe, amazement, aliveness and passion. We do not have to do anything to experience these things, except be our selves and be connected to our hearts.

When an event occurs that threatens the connection to our hearts, we experience it as shock of separation in the form of fear, and we naturally attempt to reconnect to our heart, express that disconnection, or act on the event that we experience as disruptive, through our anger, so that harmony can be restored. This is why people can get angry at a door when they stub their toe. The release helps them to express their pain so that they can get past their hurt and reconnect to the state they were before the incident happened. Our natural process seeks to immediately heal our disconnection.

We see this process with young children. They run to their parents when they hear the clap of thunder during a storm, because they are afraid. The sound startled them and disturbed their connection to their core. What they seek from their parent's love is closure. When the parent hugs them, and lets them know they're loved and protected, the show of love invites the child to return to his own heart. The disconnection and fear are healed.

Now, let us look at what happens when that child does not heal. Let's look at the sequence that creates emotions.

The sequence of forming an emotion

Although we are using a young child and their fear of lightning as an example, this sequence is typical for many of us. See if you can identify some of your own patterns or of those around you.

1. The will acts to reconnect to the heart.

The running towards the parents is the child's demonstration of the need for closure. It is an expression of the child's will to heal his fear.

2. When a fear is not healed, it is held.

Imagine that there is no parent to hug the scared child. There is no closure. Perhaps the parent says to the child "*You are too old to be afraid!*" What does the child do? Often children hold onto their fear until such time as healing can take place. They may seek that healing from the other parent. Or they may hold that fear for many years, until it is healed.

3. The will acts through our feeling of anger.

When the will to heal is frustrated, because the hug was refused, then it may express itself as anger. That anger may act to make the parents take notice. The child may insist, demand or express his need and frustration.

4. The frustrated will begins to be disowned.

The will that originally expressed itself in action, by coming to the parents and then as anger to get their attention, begins to focus on the parents' responsibility to make the desired changes. The child may now wait for the parents to respond or change their attitude so that the healing the child originally sought can take place.

The problem is that the child begins to give away his own responsibility for healing. The child divests his own responsibility for healing, and from a reactive stance, makes the parents totally responsible. The frustrated will is disowned, and attached to someone else – "*It is their fault!*"

By making the parents totally responsible, the child is no longer focused on or willing to heal himself. Now, instead, his ability to be healed depends on a desired change in the parents.

5. The blame seals the emotion.

Blaming the parents justifies holding the hurt and separation from the heart, because from the child's point of view, the parents can do something about it and they won't. From the child's point of view, the parents don't love him. From the child's point of view, he has every right to be angry with them because they have actively ignored his feelings, frustration and fear. The child senses he is justified in not owning responsibility for the loss of his own will in the form of anger. His disconnection from his heart is no longer his responsibility, it is theirs. It's the parents' fault!

The child holds a grudge. The child blames his parents for his disconnection from his own heart and for his anger. Now the experience of disconnection has a charge. It has become an emotion.

6. The power is transferred to others.

Now, the child waits for the parents to change their behavior before he can release the emotional charge. It's up to them now. They have the power. They have to notice that the hurt is being held. They have to do something about it. They are responsible for what happened!

7. The emotions wait to be triggered.

When the emotion is triggered in some way, the fear, anger and blame may rise to the surface again. What forces the emotions to the surface is the pressure to heal. However, as long as the child holds blame and as long as the parents are made responsible, healing is pushed aside. Instead, what takes center stage is the demonstration of hurt, frustration and anger that holds the separation the child experiences from his heart over the issue.

We are using an imaginary child to show how emotions form. The same pattern could just as easily have happened with an adult. The process is similar, because its roots are in childhood. This is why emotions, for the most part, are childish. It is their nature.

Share your feelings, don't share your emotions

Emotions make a mess of things. Trying to deal with them, talking about them or expressing them only strengthens them. The more we blame others, the less likely they are to help us. The more we give away our will in the form of anger and emotions, the more powerless we make ourselves.

Because emotions hold our disconnection from our hearts and our will, when they come to the surface, or are triggered, they often take over the moment. They surface in full fury and justification, because underneath them is held the need to reconnect. It is a life need. Unfortunately, whereas our immediate feelings of disconnection can save us, our emotions can only sink us.

Emotions re-connect us to the wound that created them. That is all they do! This is the big difference between feelings and emotions. Feelings connect us to our heart. Emotions connect us to our wound and to our experience of disconnection from our heart. This is why it is best to leave emotions alone. Many hours and even years of therapy can be wasted talking over and indulging in emotions. You cannot get rid of emotions by giving them energy or focus. This direction only strengthens them, and more importantly, strengthens their hold over your life. The only way to deal with emotions is to bypass them and find another way to reconnect with your heart, directly.

Emotional states

Our emotions join over time to form patterns and emotional states. Emotional states not only hold our separation from our hearts and our will, they also define us. We give them the power to define us because we are avoiding the cluster of fears and experiences of disowned will that our emotions contain.

We may identify ourselves as being unloved, rejected or outraged and interact with others from that stance, regardless of what they do. Or, we may see ourselves as nice, deserving and respected. We may try very hard to maintain that image of ourselves. However, whether they are looked at as positive or negative, ultimately, emotional states hold us back.

In this way, we are pulled to adapt to false beliefs about ourselves that have arisen through past experiences where we gave away our will in connection to our core.

Now, these emotional states act like a false core, like a false image of ourselves that we hold on to, because we are afraid to let go. They define us.

Positive emotional states
"I must be good because they tell me so"

It is easy to see how negative emotional states hold us back. How is it that positive states hold us back or are not good for us? Let's take a look at a few examples. See what you think.

One positive emotional state is that of the 'nice guy or good girl.' Have you encountered people that identify with that state? They always try to be 'nice,' polite, and sweet. It is not so much what they do that is the problem; rather, it is what they don't do.

'Nice' people do not use their power. As a result 'nice' people do what others want, even when it goes against what they feel, want, or need. Being 'nice' for them means being accepted and this acceptance is more important than their love for themselves; it is more important then their connection to their own heart, to their integrity and self-honesty.

As a result, 'nice' people can be extremely dangerous, because their need to be nice is open to manipulation. There is a fairly well-known piece of research called the Milgram experiment,[2] first described in 1963 by Stanley Milgram, in which the experimenter ordered participants to give what they believed to be increasingly painful and dangerous electric shocks to other subjects, who were actually actors. In spite of their conflict with doing so, they did as instructed.

Still not convinced that identification with positive emotional states is not good for you? Let's look at what can happen when we identify with some commonly accepted positive states like being generous or gifted. Read on.

Do you think you are generous? Some people give out of embarrassment or guilt, yet they hold on to a self-image of generosity that makes it difficult for them to refuse giving money to others. Their generosity does not come from their heart but from their fear. Acting on such a false generosity will not reconnect them to their heart or free them of their fear. So they give, but get little back in return.

Parents often seek to be proud of their children. Sometimes, they may convince the children that they are gifted in some way. When children identify with being gifted under these circumstances, they hold on to a lie about themselves, in order to be loved. The consequence of that 'positive' definition of themselves is the potential for years of suffering and disappointment they may experience in fulfilling or maintaining that wrong self image.

I remember a case where a parents was so proud of their 'gifted' child that they lied to others of their daughter's achievement. Those lies hurt their daughter's self-esteem, because she did not get acknowledged for what she actually achieved.

In another case, the child underwent hours of extra tutoring and homework each week, in order to support his parents' deception that he was a 'bright child.' When he attended university, he failed miserably, because the academic life was never what suited him.

Sugarcoated disconnections

Positive emotional states do not connect you to your feelings, nor to your heart, but to something else. They reinforce your disconnection from feeling and will. In a way, you can look upon positive states as sugarcoated disconnections. They are often handles that parents, and later your friends, can use on you in order to get what they want from you. The trick is, you are convinced it is also what you want.

Your friends brand you as being loyal, and it becomes part of your self-esteem. They intend to do something that goes beyond what you are willing to do. When you go against their wishes, you are accused of being disloyal.

Even though emotional states can appear positive, they actually limit or narrow your experience. They limit you because they define who you are or what you may experience. They limit you because you try to achieve the goal of that state rather than reconnection with your heart and integrity.

Emotional states also limit you in a way that is more subtle. You are asked to perform an action, to do something, or be something, in order for acceptance or approval to occur. The hidden message is, "*You are not acceptable as you are.*"

The wrong journey for acceptance

In many traditions, it is important, when entering a room or beginning a journey, to literally start on the right foot. It is a reminder to be aware of why and for whom you are acting and for whom you are initiating an effort. When that step is made for the wrong reasons, when it is a false step, then that journey may be a lot of effort lost.

I know of many people who studied in college or university and received degrees that they never used. Instead of following their hearts, some followed the wishes of their parents. Others took the courses that seemed easier or safer for them at the time. The goal was to get a degree, to be perceived of as a 'success.' All ended up owing a great deal of money. Some ended up in very low paying jobs, because they never sought the skills to make a comfortable living. Instead, they sought acceptance from others. That effort could have been more fruitful if they had accepted themselves at the beginning, if their first step was in the direction of their own heart, and towards what was good for them.

Many institutions of higher learning have in their motto, or above their entrance, the expression "Know thyself." Unfortunately, many people are convinced that they already know themselves as defined by an emotional state — nice, good, smart, generous, uncomplaining, helpful, useful and the like. The positive emotional states are not you. In fact, they hide you from you. It is not in your best interests to move closer to something that defines you and limits your own aliveness.

Your journey in life is to reveal your authentic self. It is a journey you have to do for yourself. Our journey in life is not for the 'nice guy or gal' to be improved upon. It is instead a journey we have to make for our true selves.

Negative emotional states

We are all familiar with the negative emotional states of abandonment, failure or guilt. These emotional states have a strong hold because in effect they put you down for being separated from your heart. In that way, negative emotional states place a large impediment in the way of your reconnection.

Unlike a positive emotional state that often requires action to achieve its benefits or pay off, a negative emotional state puts you down regardless of what you do. A negative emotional state continues to define you as being separated from your heart, until you overcome its hold on you.

For example, people that hold a negative emotional state of being fat continue to hold that self-image even while they're losing weight. In extreme cases, people have starved themselves, because regardless of their dieting, or even looking in the mirror, they did not switch off their negative self image or negative emotional state.

Breaking free from emotional states

So the question is, what can you do about emotional states? How can you break out of a pattern that defines you in this limiting way? The solution is in two parts.

Part 1: Becoming more important than your emotional state

You must choose to be more important than your limiting state or belief. The power the limiting state has over you is that it defines you; it determines that you are less important than the state. You need to reverse that. One way that you can re-establish your importance is in telling yourself the truth. There is a saying, *"The truth will set you free."* The truth here is what re-connects you to the freedom of your heart:

- If the emotional state is telling you that you need to be a nice guy, then you need to tell yourself that you have the power and right to follow your own heart.

- If your emotional states are telling you that you are fat, you need to tell yourself that you are okay and have worth as you are. A person who feels worthy and accepts themselves has an easier time losing weight.

- You need to tell yourself that you are successful, because a successful person will reach for success.

- You need to tell yourself that you are loved when you hear your emotions tell you otherwise.

- You need to counter the lies that your disconnections tell you, because they speak from disconnection.

- You need to speak the words of connection that lead you back to healing. Find your own appropriate words and truth and begin to set yourself free.

Believe it or not, this process can be powerfully transforming. You may think that simply correcting yourself after putting your self down, and saying something positive to lift yourself up, is not a big deal. It is a big deal.

One of the secrets of taking such an action is that you are re-engaging your will and placing it back into the equation. As long as you fall for the limiting definitions of yourself, you are falling for the abandonment of your will. Bring your will back into your life. You must be greater than the useless limiting definitions of who you are. Say so. Speak up for yourself!

Part 2: Caring for your heart instead of the emotional state

Real success comes when you can reestablish your connection to your heart and to your true feelings. You have to risk for your heart. You have to risk that you care enough for yourself and for your feelings.

Often, with emotional patterns and states, there is a habit of not taking care of feelings and the heart. This has to be reversed through actions. These actions may involve asking for what you want. It may involve taking care of your feelings by acknowledging or expressing them when someone is negative towards you. It may involve not reacting to what others say or do, but acting out of your heart, acting to regain your connection to your heart.

Often, what needs to be built up is trust. As you trust yourself, and trust your freedom to express and to take care of your feelings, then emotional states have less control in your life. This is because their power comes from your lack of trust in yourself.

In order to break out of the hold of emotions, you must make the efforts that connect you directly to your heart. It does not matter that you once got hurt when not taking care of your feelings. It does not matter that you once got hurt when you asked for what you wanted. What matters is what you do today. Every time you risk taking care of your feelings and every time you risk asking for what you want, you move one step closer to your heart, and more importantly, to trusting that it is okay to be as you are and to be connected to your heart.

You must do this for yourself. No one else can do this for you. People can help you get close. They can support you. They can encourage you. But this you must do for yourself. You must do those positive actions that reconnect you to your heart. All of your emotions are vestiges of times when that connection did not happen. You must stop celebrating these disconnections. You must begin to connect. Every time you risk expressing your feelings as you are, every time you risk asking for what you want in your heart, every time you resist shrinking from what people may say of you and instead choose to stand up for your own worth — it sends a powerful message throughout your whole being: "*It is now okay to be alive for myself, it is okay to feel, it is okay being in my heart, and it is okay to be centered!*" In the chapters that follow, we will be looking at ways to do just that.

A leap of faith

They say a long journey begins with a single step. The step of taking care of your feelings, or your best interests or your heart, only looks like a step. It is actually a leap of faith. It is stretching your trust in yourself toward being greater than the limitations you have been carrying. In this leap of faith, you are being asked to let go of those limitations. You're being asked to let go of the negative definitions of who you are. You are asked to let go of the fear that asking for what you want will get you rejected. You are asked to let go of the fear that if you take care of your feelings, you will not be liked or loved. When you can risk these limitations, and demonstrate that you value yourself more than your fears, you demonstrate your courage and heartfulness. You demonstrate that you are the center of your life, not your fears. That leap of faith in yourself lands you in your heart. That demonstration of action for yourself strengthens your trust in yourself.

The real magic

When the dust settles, the real magic is that the young part of you, your inner child, witnesses that you are finally taking care of yourself at the level of feelings; that you love yourself and are supporting your expansion into the world. That little one has been holding on to the key of your own joy and power. That original part of you has always been there, inherent in your feelings and in your heart.

The key that the little one holds is trust. Once you have demonstrated that your heart and spontaneity can trust that you are taking care of them, joy and power begin to flow through your being. Only lack of trust held you back. Your courage now begins to flow out of your heart through actions with others.

Your self-worth begins to flow out of your throat as the resonance and effectiveness of your words. Encouragement begins to flow out of the sparkle of your eyes to the people around you. Your freedom flows in living your own life fully. You are pulled to being centered. And in the process you pull others towards you, because they want to bask in the same aliveness that you have welcome back to your life; because being centered and being in your heart is positively contagious.

Chapter summary

In this chapter, we looked at the feelings of joy, fear and anger and the means to return to joy, to overcome fear and anger through reconnecting with our hearts and by taking care of our feelings.

We also looked at how emotions and emotional states form and the means of overcoming them through reintroducing our will.

A summary of the process by which emotions and emotional states form and an overview of feelings, emotions and states are found in the Appendix as *Feelings Emotions and States: A Summary.* In addition, there is a table to help the reader see the differences at a glance.

A more detailed list of feelings, emotions and states is found in the Appendix as *Feelings Emotions and States: A Listing.* Take time to browse through the lists. See if you can spot some of your tendencies, or the tendencies of those that are around you.

How Did We Lose Our Inner Child?

In the previous chapter we looked at how emotions and emotional patterns are ways that we maintain our separation from our heart. It is not the whole story. There is something else that contributes to our separation from who we are, and in some ways, it has to do with love: whom we love, whom we are loved by, and the sacrifices we are willing to make to be loved.

If you watch a healthy young child you will see someone excited and full of life. They express their own feelings, joy and enthusiasm and seek out positive interactions with others.

So the question is, as this child grows up, why would they lose that connection to their joy, wonder and aliveness?

The new clothes

Let's go back to where it all began for us, to earlier experiences.

You start out in life primarily in-the-moment with your feelings and experience. There is no sense of past or future, no sense of holding on to your experiences, or bringing something forward from the past, or delaying gratification until some future time.

These things are learned.

As children, our experience of being in the world includes our own joy and enthusiasm. We are fascinated with life. We seek out positive interactions with others. Where we have been encouraged, we may have felt supported in developing our own sense of importance, of being effective and of making a difference with the people we love and in the world of our experience. In this manner, we share our joy of being, and of being with others.

These experiences may stretch us, ask us to expand, to grow and extend our horizons as we extend ourselves into the world. Although at times we may be pulled from our relationship to our own core, we are still connected and return there easily, with little effort.

If you watch carefully the way an infant interacts with a parent, you will see numerous messages, communications and interactions occurring, in every moment. These include a multitude of physical cues and later, eye contact, touching, the sound of the beating of the hearts, voice, gestures and so forth.

At the beginning of the interaction, there is a flood of information and attention, and most infants crave this. The infant has basic physical needs, many of which need the attention of the parent. There is symbiosis in that the child offers their innocent connection to being in-the-moment and to joy, and the parent offers their love sustaining the child's ability to be in that state.

When others start to define us

As a child, you began to unfold to the experiences around you and to interact with the people in your life: your parents and family, and later your friends or others. These are the people with whom you share love and heart. Out of love, you move outwardly and open up to them. You learn through them. You may even allow them to define who you are. You may be willing to shift toward them, in the direction that they want you to be. In a sense, you are willing to be defined by their hearts. To the degree that you shift toward the significant people in your life, you are also at risk of being drawn away from your own center and your own authenticity, in order to accommodate your relationship to them.

As you adapt to your family and world, you are pulled out of a simpler relationship within yourself and the world, into a more complex relationship that layers your experiences and identifications of who you are in the world. This process can be an unfolding of your potential into the world; a means by which you learn to become a competent and active participant in what life has to offer.

This process can also be a contraction of your experience of the present moment and connection to joy. The way this occurs has great bearing on how you see yourself, how you see others and how you tend to diminish who you really are.

Wearing clothes that don't fit

The interaction between a parent and their child, draws the infant out. However, a parent seldom approaches a child as he or she is. More often, the child is approached with a parent's own preconceived ideas, expectations and hopes, or with the parent's reaction or response to what the child has done. It is difficult to always be in a great mood while changing diapers, cleaning the carpet from splattered food, or after an episode where the infant acted in a way that may have caused severe injury to themselves or damage to the home. Increasingly, the parent may place responsibility for actions on the infant, before the infant is actually capable of knowing what he or she did or what is going on.

From the point of view of being the child, however, you may encounter and interpret such experiences as indicating that what you offer, and in fact who you are, may not be completely accepted or appreciated by others whom you have made important to yourself. As a result, you may contract inwardly and outwardly, or feel that you were too full of yourself, or unrealistic with what you had to offer.

That contraction happens to your flow, to your ability to

be fully present in-the-moment and to the experience of your own joy. It affects your willingness to risk being yourself, to feel powerful in the world around you, and ultimately to take responsibility for your own being. That contraction decreases your connection to your heart and to your center.

You experience the pain of that separation as fear, as a loss of energy and a loss of self esteem. You react to regain your connection through anger and through seeking attention or closure. You may seek to impress others, to change their minds about yourself or you may even perform according to their standards and expectations of you, so that ultimately you can be accepted again for who you are.

If you seek acceptance outwardly, the unfortunate consequence is that you may never gain that feeling of acceptance. Instead, you experience being pulled away from your authenticity and towards being what others want. Instead of being in touch with your core, with your truth and how you really feel, you begin to focus on the other person, their needs and their view of the world and of yourself. You begin to ignore your true feelings in order to avoid further disappointments.

This process takes you away from acting from your own authenticity, from your own truth, and from your own experience and sense of passion. It leaves you off balance and at risk of repeating the same process over and over again. This happens because you are trying to be what you are not; the clothes don't fit.

The consequence of wearing clothes that don't fit

When there is conflict, or when the children and parents are not in tune with each other, children tend to perceive this as something not supported about them, as something they are doing wrong and often, later as their fault. There tends to be a strong egocentricity in younger children in this respect.

Children experience a strong pull towards becoming what their parents reinforce and toward being in tune with their parents. What is not in tune with what the parents support is often pushed away and even denied by the children about themselves.

Over time, children tend to develop an extension out of their core, in the direction of their parents' support and recognition. This is the adapted child and personality. This extension forms an outer layer, around the core, and it is from this layer that the child increasingly chooses to interact with others.

For many children, this is the part that grows to be recognized by the parents as being their child. This is the part acknowledged, appreciated and reprimanded.

The degree to which children identify with this part of themselves, and abandon their core, defines how much they limit their experience of time, the richness of being in the moment for themselves and their joy.

A child's adaptation to a false sense of who he is, determines whether he continues to adapt to the needs of others later as an adult, or whether he can maintain and hold his own experience and power.

Healing the clothes instead of the child

You may be familiar with the story of the emperor and his new clothes. In that story, the emperor walked around naked until someone made him realize that his new clothes did not exist, and that he had been tricked.

Ironically, it is the exact opposite of what happened to most of us while growing up. To use the analogy of the emperor's story, we were told to put on the 'clothes' of being what others wanted us to be, and we were told that these 'clothes' fitted us better if we became 'invisible', if we pushed aside our true nature. Only later in life do we realize that we have also been tricked. Our adapting to what others wanted has worked against us.

It is that adapting to what others want that steals the opportunity for healing as you are. Instead, much of the time, it is the artificial adapting to what others want of you that is 'healed'. It is like asking the child to fit in the clothes instead of making the necessary alterations to the clothes to better fit the child. How often do we hear parents tell their children that it is not like them to disobey, or to run around the house or to play in front of company? How often do we hear expressions like "*children should be seen and not heard?*"

Instead of being visible as themselves, children learn to adapt, to hide behind their 'clothes'. They learn to make concessions and adjustments to their nature in order to support what 'clothes' their parents placed on them.

It is interesting to observe the real clothes that children are forced to wear. How often we see children wearing clothes that are neatly ironed and easily ruined by any child with any spirit to play and 'get dirty' as children need to do. How often we see children wearing the clothes that make them look like a miniature grown-up, when they need to be given the space and clothes to grow and be real children.

Discarding old clothes

Over time, if you still do not feel accepted for who you are, or for who you have become, you may continue to seek this acceptance from the people in your life.

The problem for most of us is that we are still trying to gain acceptance for how we have adapted, not for who we truly are. We are still trying to wear the same old clothes that never fitted us and that do us no good.

Usually, you are not aware of how much this drains your energy, or how much it separates you from your true core. You may also not be aware of how much this can confuse the people in your life and put a strain on your relationships. In this respect, and without even realizing it, you may be trying to get people to accept you in being unauthentic and contracted. And of course, if they refuse, you get 'hurt.'

Your friends and those that truly care about you may in effect be telling you that the 'clothes' you are wearing don't fit you or suit you anymore.

It's time to get rid of these useless things!

Healing the child

More often than not, trying to solve past issues in the present can lead to frustration, until you begin to understand that what you are still seeking is reconnection to your heart. You are still seeking the aliveness of your inner child.

In order to reestablish that relationship, you need to reconnect with your feelings. You need to acknowledge your true needs, your experiences, your dreams and your own spontaneous freedom. In taking responsibility for your freedom, you naturally begin the process of acting more from who you are, and you let go of making the other person responsible for your issues, your history and your healing process.

By taking care of your own process, your feelings and experience, you begin to feel safe to expand outwardly from your own space, with your own expression, and you are in a stronger position to feel joy and to be accepted by others.

> *It takes courage to push yourself to places that you have never been before... to test your limits... to break through barriers. And the day came when the risk it took to remain tight inside the bud was more painful than the risk it took to blossom.*
>
> Anais Nin

Chapter summary

In this chapter we looked at how we adapt in order to reach and receive the love of our parents. In the process of this adapting, we risk the love of others being more important than the love for ourselves, and we risk becoming what others want and not what we need to be.

To look further into how we continue to form the layers of our personality, you will find a whole chapter on the subject entitled *Forming Layers: The layers of personality and identification* in the Appendix near the end of the book.

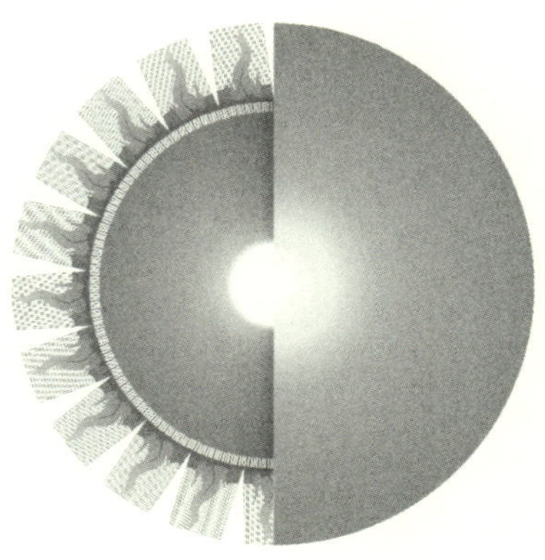

Young Face, Old Face

Your Postures in Life

Your posture is important. It affects your stance in the world. Your posture is a consequence of your state and it communicates your state to others. At the same time, when you act to change your posture, you can modify how you feel and respond. The intricate interplay between feeling, response and posture was made clear for me when I observed people posing.

Many years ago, for a summer job, I used to draw pastel portraits in shopping malls and tourist areas. It was an interesting occupation requiring great focus and awareness. I found that to truly represent a person on paper, I had to tune in to them and allow myself and my skill to be an instrument that revealed the person, in order for the drawing to be successful.

Early on, I learned an important lesson. I learned that when you are drawing a portrait of someone, you are actually drawing two portraits - a left side and a right side - seemingly two different personalities that combine subtly to create one face. Assuming that they are right-handed, the left side appears younger while the right side appears older. To do justice to a portrait, to capture the person and their energy, I had to pay special attention to both sides, and capture each. Otherwise, the result would appear hollow, un-integrated and lifeless.

This is part of the reason why some people, in order to appear glamorous, will draw a 'beauty mark' above their lip on one side of their face. They are making the two sides look more different from each other. It is the interplay of both sides of the face, and the subtle difference between them, that makes a face interesting.

One pastel portrait session stands out in my recollection. The portrait requested was of a young girl, about 6 years of age. I had agreed to do the portrait in the family's home, at the end of the day. The mother sat the daughter down on a chair, gave her a few instructions, and then proceeded to 'backseat drive' the session. This was too annoying, so I asked the father to stay, and the mother to prepare some tea, outside of the room. The daughter was very well behaved and rather quiet, especially since the portrait took about half an hour. After the mother left the room, the child's face relaxed and her eyes brightened up.

When the drawing was finished, I called in the child's mother so that I could show it to both parents. I was excited with this particular portrait, because it really worked! The child's energy, her aliveness and presence just shone out of the paper. It was more than just a likeness — it had her spirit.

The mother, however, was disappointed. For her, this was not what the child looked like at all. She could not relate to the spark in her daughter's eyes. What was sad to see, was how the right side of the child's face resumed its earlier stiffness during this conversation, and how the spark in her left eye was gone! It was as if a switch was turned off. It was clear that the child had chosen to adapt to her mother's expectations, and she did so even with her face.

This episode haunted me. When I look at faces now, I can see the history of adaptation in the left and right sides. I see people who have developed larger muscles around their right jaws, revealing years of clenching, holding themselves back and taking responsibility for others. Sometimes, there is sadness in the left eye, or a lazy left eye, as if the child side of the personality has been left behind.[3] Sometimes, the whole left face is sad or the right lip has a forced smile. They may seem happy, unless you take a second look.

I also see faces where the left and right side are balanced and in harmony with each other. Often I notice that these are faces of people that are comfortable with expressing their spontaneity and strength.

The child hiding in the left side

I use the concept 'inner child' a lot. By 'inner child,' I mean the part of us that first connected with the world and expressed enthusiasm and joy.

It is my observation that the left side of the face tends to reveal what has become of this younger and earlier part of ourselves. Not only the left side of the face, but the whole left side of the body expresses to some extent our relationship with the child-like part of our personality. If the face is sadder on this side, if the left shoulder droops a little lower, if that side of the body or the foot is planted a little further behind the right side, then here is an indication that the child side of the personality may be somewhat ignored, or held back.

The strutting of the right side

Most people are much more aware of the right side of their own face and of other people's faces, than they are of the left side of the face. It is the right side of the face that we want other's to see. If you look at traditional corporate photos, especially gallery shots, you will see, for the most part, people whose bodies are rotated, revealing mostly their right side and hiding most of their left. This is not an accident. It is the right hand that is used to greet and receive people with a hand-shake. You might, during a meeting, get a right-handed pat on the back of the right shoulder.

This is the side that acts in the world. This is the side that expresses responsibility, maturity and competence. When two people pass each other and stop to say "*Hi, how are you doing?*"

the typical focus tends to be on the right side of the upper body and head. In fact, the typical focus is often not much different from those gallery shots mentioned earlier.

Putting the faces together

If you look at people who have integrated their younger side and their older side, you may notice that the two sides look quite similar, and that the two parts look much like the whole face and personality. We have an expression *"The left hand doesn't know what the right hand is doing."* It is really a description of what happens from the perspective of integration if the two sides are not working well together. The left side is receptive, and feels, but may not know how to ask for what it wants. The right side acts, expresses, and takes responsibility but may not know what it feels. The two sides need to work together, in order to reach satisfaction and joy.

Integrating both the left and the right sides, involves taking care of our feelings. Then we can give and take, feel and act appropriately.

Our posture in life

As you may have gathered, our posture is important. It expresses our stance and how we interact with the world.

However, our posture and our stance are not just limited to the way we look. Even more important is our inner posture within our selves and with others. Are we grounded in our sense of who we are, or do we seek others all of the time to get a sense of who we are? Is our posture and our stance receptive to joy, or do we present ourselves to life closed up and fearful? Do we approach life, comfortably residing in our own hearts, open to what life offers us, or are we hiding in our heads, needing to analyze our life's every moment, before we dare let life and joy in?

In the rest of the book, we will be looking at our postures and stances to life and to ourselves that we may have chosen, or others may have chosen for us when we let them. We can change our postures. We can change our stances to life. Only we can do this for ourselves.

Chapter summary

In this chapter, we saw how we communicate our state through our face and outer posture in various ways.

We were introduced to the inner child hiding in the expression of the left side of our face and body. We also explored how we interact with our right side which typically holds our more rational and responsible expression. It is important to integrate both of these sides of ourselves.

Our posture and stance expresses how we hold our power and how we hold ourselves back. It lays the foundation for the initial impressions others have of us.

Part 2
Relationship

The Power of Relationship

Relationship is destiny

Life is an ongoing process of relationship. Where we place our focus in relationship, where we place our energy and time, directly affects us in terms of the choices we make and thus our destiny.

Our primary relationship

Our primary relationship is in our core, through our spirit. It is a relationship with our essential being, our awareness. Spiritual traditions refer to this as the Self, our Inner Light or the Universal Heart. Our experience of connecting with that being, with that state, can occur in profound moments of our lives. At such times we may experience ecstasy, unfathomable love and a profound sense of connection with the whole of the universe. More often than not, it is our heart that acts as bridge to that experience. Most of the time we experience our core being when our heart is open and we are ready to receive fully.

The inner relationship with our heart

The way to achieve that profound connection is to first establish ourselves in our heart. This is why being in the heart is so important. This is why in all spiritual traditions, the heart is emphasized. It is for this reason that the heart and being in the heart is the focus of this book. Once you have established yourself in your heart, the rest of the spiritual journey is open to you. There are many books and traditions that will help you make that journey. But first, you must start with your relationship to your own heart.

Establishing yourself in your heart brings joy and aliveness in your journey in life. It is your heart that acts as a way-station between your core and your experience in the world. It is very important to strengthen, protect and nurture your own relationship with your heart, as it is always through your heart that you extend towards outer relationships. The choice is whether you do so with an open heart or a closed heart, whether you do so by taking care of your heart or allowing yourself to get hurt.

Our outer relationship with our heart

As our awareness of our outer relationships unfolds, it captivates our attention. It pulls our love outward. As a result, we project the magic of our inner relationship onto the experience of the world around us.

Ultimately, we seek the magic of the ideal relationship that we know exists, because we have touched it in our own core. We seek it in the people we meet and in the world around us.

As children, we seek and are attracted to that ideal in our parents. We may see them as all-powerful, all-loving and all-knowing. Part of the magic we seek is our own sense of an ideal relationship. This is partly why children seek attention when they lose their inner connection. The ideal relationship they hold as their parents, helps them reconnect inwardly and with their hearts.

Later as we get older, and our relationships become more

complex, we are still attracted to finding that ideal. We are still pulled to a particular quality in someone else that reconnects us or re-establishes us with an ideal or an ideal quality inside.

In this way, we are attracted to other people. We like other people in relation to how close they are to the ideal that we seek. We dislike people and push them away when they contradict that ideal.

When we are attracted to a particular quality in someone else, that affords us the opportunity to expand our inner joy outward, we are able to bond with them. We form these bonds to the degree that we are willing to open ourselves to that person, to the degree that we are willing to share our heart and let the other into our heart. This is why, when people touch us deeply, we are letting them be in our inner relationship and are willing to let ourselves be in theirs.

The magic of such a relationship is that there is support for the experience of the inner relationship expressing itself outwardly. We experience this as 'being in love.' We experience this in the way the world holds joy for us, how everything becomes richer, more vibrant and alive for us. Our experience of being fully in the world with our inner relationship is an experience of intimacy.

However, we sometimes forget that all joy comes from within us and not from outside of us. If we forget this, then, when our outer experiences and relationships begin to crumble, we are at risk of trying to fix them instead of ourselves.

Relationship and attunement

The cohesive factor that underlies most relationships is the degree of attunement. People are attracted to each other, or form cooperative associations, to the degree that they can relate to each other, to the degree that they can tune into each other. In our culture, the ideal relationship involves attraction and bonding where two people are so much in tune with each other that they seem to act like one inseparable being.

It is rare to find everything in such positive harmony.

Instead, the cohesiveness that brings many couples together is their personal history of mutual difficulties or issues. Both people may have had similar experiences of pain or disappointment in growing up, and now they can sympathize, understand, or identify with the other person's state or experience. This makes it feel safer to open up to a receptive heart or a kindred spirit.

Negative relationships

Relationships work when there is a give and take; when there is a flow of love or energy between people. They run into difficulty when that love or flow of energy is not experienced or is interrupted for whatever reason.

Some relationships form when one partner is in need and the other is willing to give. Often what causes such a partnership to fail is this very dependency upon another person. That dependency allows at least one of the partners to remain out of their center.

For example, someone does not take responsibility to look after his own interests. Instead, he pulls on the energy and love of his partner. It is very much like a theft of energy, of resources, enthusiasm, attention, joy, love or power.

His partner, on the other hand may feed off of her sense of being nice or good. Her own sense of giving may fulfill her emotional needs of being helpful, caring and loving. Unfortunately, this stance only feeds her definition of herself. It may not feed her heart. What she may experience instead is that her true needs in relationship and in life are not being met, and that over time, her energy is being lost.

Often both partners are caught in this dance keeping them from moving forward, because it holds both from being in their hearts. This form of exchange essentially acts like a hook; one partner is caught by her own process in giving, the other in receiving. There is a net drain of effort for the giving partner. However, the receiving partner is drained in the process of not taking responsibility, in maintaining all of the hooks to get what he needs and wants, and even in 'strutting his weakness like a hammer.' The receiving partner also gets drained by not learning to hold on to what he receives. In fact, both partners get drained by not acting out of their hearts directly, and both tend to participate in this pattern until one of the partners takes responsibility for himself or herself.

People also get caught in negative relationships because of the wounds that they carry. Their past hurtful experiences can make them so sensitive to the needs of others that they focus on taking care of others and not themselves. They may seek out relationships in order to find someone who will help them heal these wounds. More often than not, relationships based on these needs are doomed to failure. Why? You cannot make someone else responsible for your life. You cannot make someone else responsible for your heart and joy. It is when you take responsibility for your life and your heart that you make yourself ready to share that heart and be fully open to relationship.

Whom do you serve?

Many of us over time, begin to focus more and more on outer relationships, and we begin to ignore our inner state, our inner relationship with our selves. It seems as if all of the action and excitement is happening out there, and to be a player, to belong and to be accepted, demands that we shift our focus outwards.

Often this process of being pulled outwards and away from our center is accelerated when we are not grounded on our inner sense of value, and instead, we seek value from others. To the degree that we do not value ourselves, we are at risk of attracting bad company, or of paying too high a price for acceptance. Under these circumstances, instead of serving and expressing our own joy, we end up serving the joy and expression of others.

Re-establishing relationship

When our interactions with others run into difficulty, it is our primary or inner relationship that is being ignored, sacrificed or pushed aside. This disconnection to our inner relationship shows up as loss of energy and enthusiasm.

Unfortunately, instead of realizing what has happened we seek to solve the problem on the outside. We seek changes in the way people interact with us and we often blame them if we feel less joy. We say things like, *"You made me feel bad."* We wait to receive the valuing and connection through others, that we have disconnected to within ourselves. We tend to force changes that we expect will make things better, by improving or changing something in our interactions with others. We say things like, *"I need for you to show me that you care,"* or *"I need to feel valued by you."*

This often doesn't work. In fact, it makes things worse and drains even more energy. Why? Because we are trying to make someone else responsible for our feelings and our state. We are setting ourselves up for being affected by and reacting to what others do. We are setting ourselves up to be the victim.

In order for you to reestablish relationship, it is necessary to reconnect with your own core and your own heart. You have to act for your heart and your feelings. Only then can you find out what you are seeking and what is not working for you. Once you have re-established that primary connection with your own heart and feelings, you will know what you want and need with others. You will know what you are seeking. Your re-connection to your own heart will make it possible to re-establish real relationships with others.

Asking for what you want

The truth is, if you do not love yourself, it is difficult to love someone else, or for them to love you. And, if you loved yourself, you would more likely know what you wanted and you would be able to ask for it.

Many people find it difficult to ask for what they want or need. Instead, they expect the other person to just 'know.' Many relationships struggle, especially early on, because people are indirect. People say things like *"If you truly loved me, then you would know what I want!"*

One form of being indirect in asking is to offer to others what you actually want for yourself. This does not work, because in offering to others what you want, people are not getting something that they want for themselves. They are getting what you want! As a result, they feel ignored or rejected. Therefore, instead of drawing them closer, you end up pushing them away!

I once knew a couple whose sex life seemed to be at an impasse. The husband was demonstrative and physical, while his wife treated him very gently and softly. They were both frustrated, until they realized that he wanted her to be more physical with him, and what she desired was softness and gentleness.

People are often indirect because they feel that if they ask directly, they will be turned down. So, they avoid the experience of disappointment. That is what happened to this previous couple. He was afraid to ask for what he wanted. He assumed that her focus on being soft and gentle meant that if he asked for something more physical, he would be rejected. His wife did the same thing. She assumed that his focus on being more physical meant that if she asked for a softer approach towards herself, she would be rejected.

The problem is that when people ask indirectly, they have already embraced the expectation of disappointment, and this is what is communicated to the partner. Being indirect, in essence, transfers the will to the other person and makes them responsible to figure it out — to determine what it is that you want and to offer it.

Know this: People do not want to support or share in your expectation that you will not get what you want. They do not want to take responsibility for your fears, and usually they do not want to waste time figuring out what you want if you refuse to ask directly. All of these things push people even further away from you and from what you want.

This kind of indirect pattern is left over from childhood, from expecting the parents to know what it is that you want and what is beneficial for you. To break through this pattern, you have to risk asking for what you want. Otherwise, this issue will just grow, forming a wedge in the relationship.

How to ask for what you want

If asking directly for what you want seems too difficult, then it may be helpful to break down the process into smaller practical steps:

Step 1: Find out what you really want.

Are you hiding behind what you are asking for? Are you asking for something that only represents or takes the place of what you really want? Are you really seeking love, attention, acknowledgment, acceptance, or encouragement? Are you seeking an opportunity to play? Are you asking for a sign that it is safe to be open and spontaneous? Find out. Contemplate. What does your own joy seek to manifest in this relationship? What do you actually desire? And what do you think will get this for you?

Step 2: Determine how to ask for what you really want.

Is the way you ask coming out of your own joy and spontaneity? Does it acknowledge another person's free choice to be in theirs?

It is very important that you ask in a way that is honest and clean, and that what you ask for does not lay blame or unrealistic responsibility on the other person. Carefully look at how you ask. Does your asking go something like this?

"You never do this."

"I can't ask for what I want because I know you're not interested."

"I have already asked so many times and nothing happened."

"You ought to know."

"Why do I need to ask?"

Do you find yourself laying blame when you ask? Do you find yourself getting in a low blow every time you ask? Do you try to get even for all those times that you didn't get what you wanted? Is your asking thinly disguised complaining? All of these ways of 'asking' are ways to make sure it doesn't happen, by alienating the other person.

The trap here is in making other people responsible for you, for what you want and for what you feel. People do not respond well when you try to steal their right to be themselves. They also do not want to take on your responsibility for being happy. If you make them responsible for your happiness, then who is the one who is going to be happy? That stance is doomed to failure.

In fact, people respond well when you ask out of your heart, out of your joy and spontaneity, and when you offer them a free choice to be in theirs. Asking is more successful when it is an invitation to share rather than an obligation, a demand or a complaint. Consider phrasing your requests in a more positive way:

"Let's try something new!"

'Would you like to share some time together?

"How do you feel about this?

"I would like to give this a try. Are you interested?

"This might be fun.

"I'm thinking of doing this. Would you like to join me?

Step 3: Reconnect to your own inner relationship.

Get in touch with your heart. What does your heart really need or want? How do you really feel, right now? What do you need to do in order to take care of yourself and your feelings, right now? Other people are not responsible for what you place in your heart. You are. So, take a good look at what you're placing in your heart. Take a good look at how you are taking care of your heart. Take the time to listen to your own heart.

It is important that you reconnect to your inner child right now. The joyful child is who others want to relate to, and that is where you need to start. Connect to that source of playfulness, spontaneity and realness that is revealed in your own heart. Acknowledge your heart and your own feelings. Acknowledge the inner child inside of you as not different from your immediate feelings and trust.

In this way, you have done your own acknowledging for yourself. You are not waiting for that acknowledgement to come from others. You have taken responsibility to be who you are. From that place, you can ask for what you want and need in a way that is no longer a demand, but is an opportunity to play and to share. Such an invitation is more likely to be heard and less likely to be refused.

Step 4: Take appropriate action from your own heart.

Sometimes, the process of asking gets stuck because the other person is waiting for you to do something. It may be that your process of asking is placing upon them the responsibility of initiating an action. It may be that for them, it is you that must act so they can respond. Therefore, find out if the impasse is an action that needs to be taken, or words that need to be said. Find out what each of you is waiting for. You may be waiting for the same thing, or one of you may be waiting for something that the other has no idea about. Find out and share.

Be direct with yourself. Be honest. Connect with your heart. Listen to your heart. Then you can be direct with people and you can be honest with them. When you approach people from the place of the heart, they are likely to respond in kind.

Chapter Summary

In this chapter we looked at relationships from the point of view of being connected to our heart. We examined ways in which we get pulled away from that primary relationship, and how we tend to seek solutions on the outside. We saw how at such times, it is our inner relationship with our core and heart that needs to be healed through our own efforts and actions. The next chapter takes us further into the journey of healing our heart.

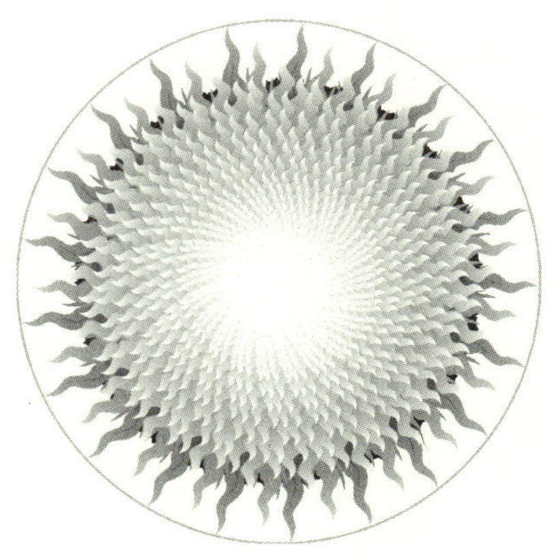

Healing the Fire Within

Revealing your Heart

This chapter takes another look at feelings and emotions, but this time from the perspective of the heart.

The freedom of the heart

If you look closely at some of the paintings from many of the world's traditions, you will likely find a depiction of the heart pictured with a light or a flame. Have you ever wondered why the flame is there and why it appears in the heart?

In our modern culture, the depiction of that same flame or light has moved from being in the heart to being in the mind or in our head. It is the image of the light bulb. The quality of inspiration that we sometimes coin with the idea of a light bulb is the freedom of thinking 'out of the box.' It is about being free of the box that our own mind creates out of fear, judgment or reaction. We often associate preparing ourselves for the moment of inspiration by surrendering our logic and allowing the answer to come from someplace else. Surprisingly, that freedom does not actually come from the mind. In fact, it is the freedom of being bathed in the light of the heart.

How we hide our freedom

If our experience of freedom lies in the heart, then it begs the question, why is it that people do not routinely find it there? To understand why, let's go back to the depiction of the light of the heart as a flame. Let's use a candle for our analogy.

Just like a candle waxes and surrounds itself with the melted wax that it did not burn off, the heart also accumulates around itself the material that has not burnt off - our hurts, disappointments and emotions. We hold on to this material in the hopes of healing it later and thus be able to return to our hearts. Meanwhile, it hides our own inner light from us, at the level of the heart.

At the physical level, the heart is the pump that sends the blood with nutrients and oxygen all over the body. At the mental, emotional and spirit levels, the heart is a generator of energy, a dynamo that brings us into being, into the present moment, into our joy, our feeling and aliveness. The connection to the heart's free and revealing light is the very source of inspiration to the mind. This is evidenced by the processes that tend to invite inspiration: meditation, contemplation, play, music and art. These experiences invite us to be present and to be open to what each moment offers us. We do not tend to be inspired by just thinking harder. Inspiration is hampered by trying to over focus on an issue, as this tends to remove us from connection to the heart. Inspiration is released when there is a relaxation and a willingness to be open, by returning to the heart. Inspiration means literally to 'in-spire,' to breathe in, to let the world in, to let life in.

This is partly why, when the flash of understanding or breakthrough occurs, we feel more joy and more exhilaration. In a very real way, the flash of inspiration expresses our reconnection to our hearts and to life.

The bon-fire of the heart

Have you ever wondered what fuel lights the heart, driving the flame of being in-the-moment and in joy? That fuel is the past. It is the previous moment. It is our ability to let go of all the residue of the previous experiences and to be open to what is offered in the present that supports that flame. This is what makes the process of confession, reconciliation and forgiveness work. When we let go of the things that hold us to the past, we become more open to receiving in the present.

There is magic in this process of letting go. Have you noticed the attraction of being around a bon-fire? The word actually goes back to the shamanic Bon tradition of pre-Buddhist Tibet. In most shamanic traditions, offerings are made to the sacred fire. The offerings can be prayers, but more often than not, what is symbolically offered in the feeding of the fire, is what is holding us back. This outer fire is a manifestation of our inner fire, of the free fire of the heart.

Making an offering with your heart

You can make an offering to the fire of your heart. You don't need to wait until you are near a bon-fire to make this offering. Any situation that is transformative will do just fine. It is the willingness and intention to be opened that matters.

One opportunity for opening the heart is familiar to most people - giving 'thanks' before eating a meal. The tradition of saying 'Grace' before meals is a way we can connect to our heart through the openness of receiving, through gratitude.

Try this practice. Before you eat, offer your thanks for the food you are about to receive. Then offer yourself. Offer that your heart may be open to receive fully what is offered. Then offer your thanks for the opportunity to receive and your gratitude for this process. In this way, through gratitude, you link the acknowledgement for what you are receiving with the openness and willingness to receive what is offered. This is true prayer.

You may want to experiment with this practice of connecting to your heart in other situations in your life; before meetings, before giving a presentation, before new experiences, even before doing things that you previously avoided. Experiment by doing this before asking for what you want. By taking the time to open your heart for your own upliftment, you prepare yourself to be more present, more alive to what life has to give you. And then, life has an amazing tendency to return your favor.

The mind in the heart

The mind's natural resting place is in the heart. It is in order to bring the mind back into the heart, that people do practices such as meditation or contemplation. The arts, music and expansive experiences such as being in nature can also bring us back to our hearts.

The consequence of having a mind that is not connected to

the heart is that it lacks the freedom to create, to think out of the box. Instead of breaking out of the box, out of a constrained line of reasoning, such a mind instead tends to recreate, making boxes within more boxes. This process leads to differentiation and specialization. Often, there is more information and detail, but not necessarily more clarity or understanding.

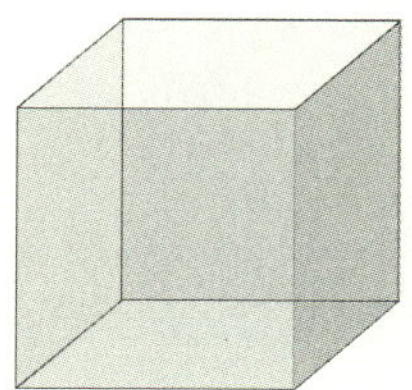

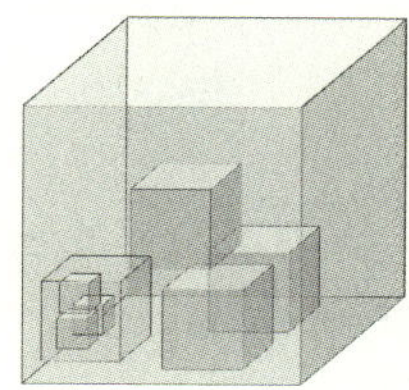

Historically, the great advances have come about when people break out of their constrained lines of reasoning and instead become open to more creative solutions and original directions.[4]

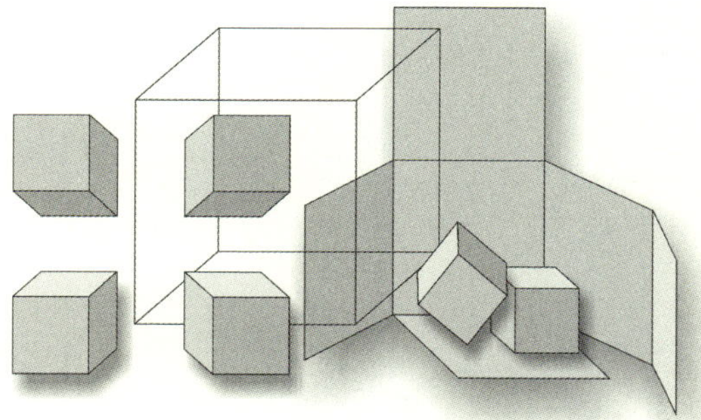

These creative advances are typically more elegant, have greater longevity and are better connected to the whole of knowledge. Unfortunately, many people choose the boxed-in way of looking at the world on the basis of fear rather than effectiveness. For most people, the constrained approach, much like holding on to a guide rope, is less scary than risking the unknown or unfamiliar.

The consequences of putting boxes around our thinking and perceptions of the world around us are limits to our freedom and opportunities. Let's take a closer look at how this happens and what we can do about it.

How does the experience of pain and disconnection constrict the mind and the heart?

To answer this question, let's look at an idealized situation of a child in relationship with others, and with his own heart. Let's take a look at what happens around the heart of this child.

When reconnection does happen:

In the process of living, this child will absorb the effects of various experiences. His more painful experiences, those that shock his system, may lead to a separation from the experience of being in the moment, of being safe and in joy. Each painful experience becomes a major center of attention. It is at this stage that a child will seek closure, connection, reconciliation or acknowledgement from his parent. The child seeks help in the process of reconnecting back to his own heart.

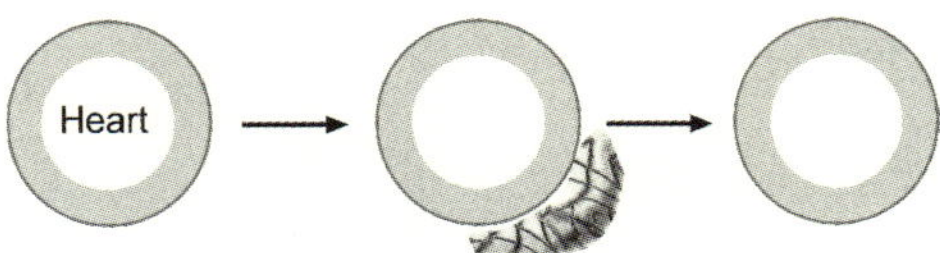

This attempt at reconnecting is an everyday occurrence. The child may cut his finger and run to the parent for a hug, for closure. A moment of heartful recognition from his parent like their kissing the child's finger and saying *"Its alright now, it's healed!"* will help bring the child back from his sense of separation and pain. He can now return to the sense that it is safe to be in the heart.

When reconnection doesn't happen:

If the attempts at reconnecting to the heart are unsuccessful, if the parent does not offer closure to the child, then the constricting experiences and their effects are held in order to be released at a later time. The child may brood, or maintain a stance of sadness, in order to bring attention back to his need for closure and thus reconnection to his heart. If there is no resolution, if reconnection does not happen, then these experiences of separation begin to cluster around the child's heart. As these clusters of wound accumulate, the mind becomes increasingly separated from the heart, and spends more time focusing on these wounds instead.

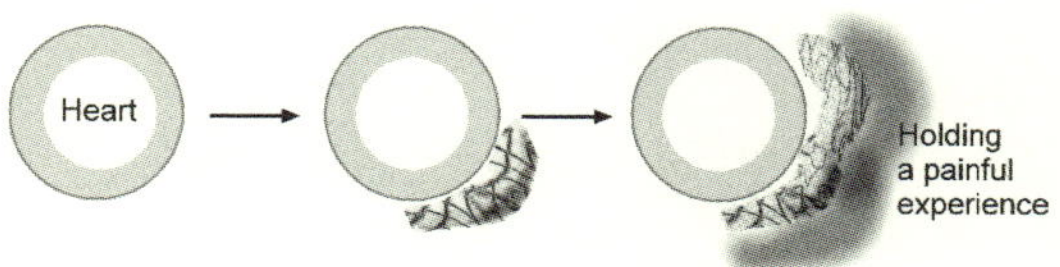

Why do we hold on to these wounds?

These wounds and experiences of separation from our heart are held for the very same reason that we seek closure in the first place. We seek to be healed, in the moment, just like the child that cut his finger sought closure, through the love of his parents.

As has been already mentioned in previous chapters, we always heal in the present moment. This is where healing always takes place. It does not take place in the past or in the future, because these are not directly connected to the heart, to the moment. This is partly why, when people recall their traumas and past hurts, this of itself does not heal them. What heals them is action in the present moment.

When healing in the present moment does not take place, we then hold on to the wounds, to the shock that separated us from our hearts, in order to be healed in the next moment. Unfortunately, the immediate opportunity for healing often passes us by, but holding the hurt continues. In this way, the child who did not receive the attention needed when he cut his finger, is likely later in life to seek attention in related ways. However, a forty year old man trying to get healed by over dramatizing a very minor injury is not likely to get what he needs!

As silly as this may sound, we try to heal old hurts in new situations in a similar manner. We often do not succeed because the new situation may not offer the conditions for healing that we need. Then, instead of healing, we add this 'new failure' to the old wound, because again, we did not get what we needed.

As these constrictions are held, often they clump around the heart, seeking the joy and freedom that the heart holds to set them free.

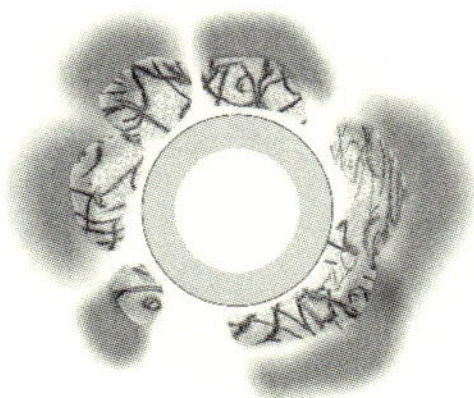

Unfortunately, the clumping of our own unresolved issues can block our direct access to our own heart. These hurts, emotional scars and wounds, are not held by our hearts. Our hearts remain free and pure. What happens is that our hurts accumulate around our hearts, and they are what we tend to encounter when we try to reconnect to our heart. In a manner of speaking, the wounds demand healing by standing in the way to our heart. As this clustering continues, we tend not to experience the world from the joy and freedom of our hearts, but from the contracted sense of ourselves held in them.

The consequence of holding our wounds

We lose much of our vital energy when we begin to focus our resources into defending and protecting ourselves from further injury. We also lose energy in the process of holding on to our hurts, instead of letting them go. Holding on to our fears constrains our energy, because fear contracts us. It decreases our willingness to be open for what life has to offer and to be more present in each new moment.

Unfortunately, holding on to our hurts also tends to push

us into recreating similar experiences that caused them in the first place. Recall the example of the forty year old man. He is likely to experience more rejection from others if he continues to act like a child, although he is still trying to heal an old childhood wound.

Often, people who have imbibed a great deal of rejection are more likely to look and walk dejected. This invites negative responses from others, perpetuating their stance. Even in anticipating negative outcomes, we contribute towards them.

Many people that carry clustering around their hearts are still waiting for a magical relationship with a parent figure that would help them heal in the manner that was denied them. As a result, they expect others to be responsible for their own healing. This is the great trap. Until we accept responsibility for the way we feel and for our past hurts, we cannot heal ourselves.

Becoming like an onion

Ultimately and over time, the clustering becomes an increasing area of identification and sense of who we are. We begin to accept and be defined by the limitations that we hold. We may even resist change or growth, because we fear losing what we begin to believe is us. We choose friends that support not only our own separation from our heart, but our accumulated storehouse of bad experiences, stories and wounds.

Over time, this old baggage that separates us from being fully in life and in our hearts forms layers, much like an onion, with layers of defensiveness protecting older wounds. This is why, when people finally make the choices to let go of their useless baggage, to move forward, that process can be referred to as 'peeling the onion.' At this stage, issues are cross-linked, and removing one layer, tends to show up another.

Peeling the onion

Working through our layers to reveal our heart is a process that takes time, patience and will. Some people have accomplished this on their own through introspection, contemplation and self-examination. Much of the work in most spiritual paths is in fact this peeling, revealing and clearing.

This work can be greatly accelerated with the help of someone skilled in the process, and someone who has undergone their own journey. At the back of the book, I have given some guidelines for finding and evaluating such help.

What often makes this journey more difficult for us is that we tend to get entangled with the consequences of the old material that we are trying to clear. Talking about the past pulls you to the past and away from the present moment where healing can take place. **Talking about feelings is not the same thing as taking responsibility or owning your feelings.** Often the defenses that are in place to protect past wounds, try to take over the healing process. For these and other reasons, skilled help can make a great difference.

Cutting the onion

With all of the entanglements of 'peeling the onion' you might be hoping that there is another way. There are, in fact several other ways to heal. I am not disregarding working through the layers. It is a very important and at times necessary process. It can however focus too much on words, ideas and knowing. Knowing is not enough. You can know yourself intimately, and still stay stuck. Action is required in order to move forward. In fact, it is appropriate action that cuts through the onion. Not thinking, but action, takes responsibility for the heart and moves us past our hurts and emotions.

In order to understand this type of action a better, let's go back to the beginning of the process. We have already looked at how children, after they experience a shock, seek out a parent in order to help them re-connect to their heart. This is the action of the child in the direction of healing. When this action fails, the child may hold the shock so that a positive healing experience can occur later. When healing does not happen, the child holds the wound.

The wound seeks release, in a manner of speaking. Unfortunately, we know quite well that the wound cannot release itself. Otherwise drunks would be instantly healing themselves every time they reveled in their drama. It doesn't happen that way, because the emotion and hurts that we hold come from a disconnection from the heart, and all we would be releasing and achieving is further disconnection. The key is re-connection.

Using re-connection to cut the onion

As previously stated, we re-connect by taking responsibility for our feelings and for our heart. We reconnect, by taking the responsibility of taking on the role of being a parent to our wounds. As long as we are waiting for someone else to save us and heal us, we hold our wounds and we do not heal. **The wounds are nothing more than held opportunities to reconnect to our hearts.** The healing is not in holding or expressing these wounds. The healing occurs when we reconnect to our hearts.

For this reason, it really does not matter much what happened to you twenty or fifty years ago. What really matters is what you are doing today, right now, to reconnect to your heart. Every time that you take care of your feelings, every time that you take responsibility for how you feel and every time you take charge of being in your heart, you move towards reconnection.

The great secret is that each time you take care of your feelings and state, you lower the hold that your previous negative experiences have on you because you do not give these experiences any more energy; you do not 'buy into' them.

Another secret is that when you act in the direction of your well being, especially with others, you signal to yourself, to your whole system, to everything that you are holding, that you are willing and able now to take care of yourself. You are letting your inner child know that the wait is over. Someone is finally taking care of you. That someone is you!

Out of that self-demonstration arises the willingness to trust that you will not get hurt the same way again, that you no longer have to hold back what you have to offer. This is how the onion is cut. So let's cut the onion with action!

In the chapters that follow, we will be looking in detail at some of these actions.

Chapter Summary

In this chapter we looked at the heart as the source of freedom and spontaneity, and as the natural resting place for our mind. We also looked at how and why we hold our wounds and how these cluster around the heart. In this chapter, the process of taking care of our feelings through responsible action was examined as a means of releasing and healing our wounds and issues.

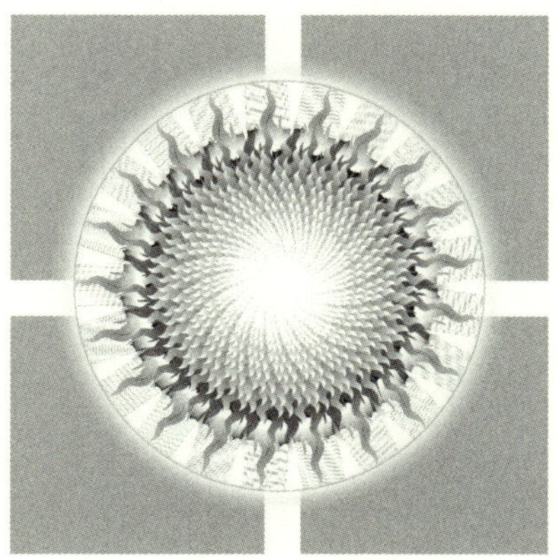

The Heart of the Matter

Recovering your heart

In each challenging event of our lives, we are presented with two things. The first is very familiar: the problem, the challenge, and the situation that makes our life difficult, or disrupts our way of being, and we just wish it would go away.

The second is a gift, an opportunity to make a shift forward towards growth. This part is often not very familiar to most of us. It asks us to go beyond our limitations and fears, and become someone greater than when we started.

It is always our choice whether we ride each event in our lives towards our hearts or away from our hearts. This is truly the choice we have in life. Our real freedom is in this choice. At each moment, with each event, we have the gift of the experience and also the consequence of avoiding the gift.

It is because many of us have become so accustomed to living away from our core that we tend to over focus on problems and issues. Instead of residing in our hearts, we spend too much time being blocked from our hearts by all of the accumulated negative emotions and hurtful experiences that form a crust around our hearts.

When the crust matters

Because we spend so much time in this crust of emotions, problems, disappointments, expectations and self judgments, they begin to matter to us, out of proportion to their value in our lives. If we have gotten used to being un-centered, very removed from the moment and not in our own hearts, we tend to perceive the world in the same way. As a result, we begin to identify with our crust, or what matters to us according to our own limitations. It is our own personal crust, our own personal materializing of the issues that we continually experience.

In this manner, we encounter our disappointments and our frustrations. We encounter the crust in life that we identify with and that we have gotten used to. As a result, we may even wonder why we are so unlucky! We may wonder why the world is treating us so unfairly! In that state, we do not notice that we are interacting with the world from our crust, not our hearts, and so we get crust in return!

What we tend to miss are the gifts hiding in those experiences. Because we are avoiding being open in our own heart, we also avoid being open to the gifts that come our way.

We did not start out this way. At first, because there may have been only several instances of this crust, we are able to reconnect to the heart. The crust only hid some of our heart from us. This is like the child that is sad one moment and happy again a few moments later.

After a time, there is an accumulation of hurts and pain around our hearts that we hold on to and do not release, and we tend to identify with these accumulated negative experiences, as if this is who we are.

We have expressions such as "*what's the matter?*" or "*what matters to me is*" or we say things like *"it doesn't matter*" when it does. Of course, the 'matter' that we are referring to is the material we have difficulty letting go of that accumulates around us, around our joy and our aliveness. As it accumulates around us, it stifles us.

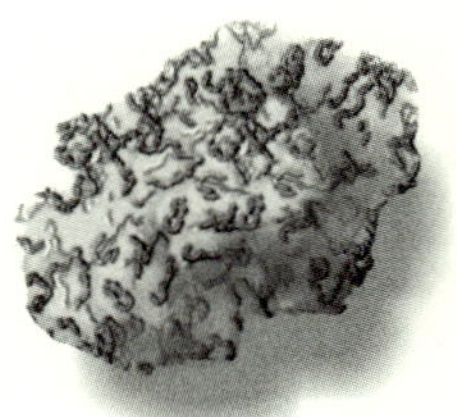

What begins to matter to us is protecting that crust around our hearts more than protecting our own hearts. We learn to avoid the pain when that crust is touched, pushed or stepped on. Our sensitivity and identification with our crust, and thus what matters to us, extends to the world around us. Ultimately, the situation develops when access to the heart, to our center of being, is blocked by that crust.

When we can not reconnect with our own hearts and to our own core, we are prone to centering on other things: our issues, our difficult memories, external objects, ideals, hopes and fears. We also try to center on the core of others. Because we are not in our hearts, it is our disowned and still hurting experiences that reach out to other people. In this way, we blame others and make them responsible for holding or taking care of our own issues.

What can save us from continuing to move further and further from our hearts and joy, are the experiences that challenge our crust, that challenge what we have come to believe matters to us.

Breaking the crust

Often, when we experience a difficult situation, the tendency is to be angry and blame someone else, someone close to us, or the universe. We tend to run from having any responsibility or part in our process. We tend to choose to play the role of the victim – *"Why has this happened to me?"*

Why do we act this way? It is because we are not responding with our hearts. Instead, our response is fueled by the encrusting of emotions and negative experiences that is far removed from our heart. In this crust are buried all the angers we have not released; the rage we deny, our frustrations and confusion. From this place we react with an emotional charge, with the same denial, rage or confusion. We say things like *"This can't be happening,"* or *"If there is a creator, how could they let this happen?"*

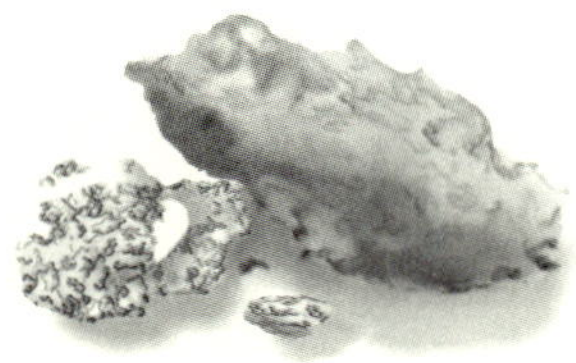

However, that same difficult or challenging experience can also bring attention to what really matters. During these times, people have the opportunity to break the crust of their pride, arrogance, conceit, self-delusion or avoidance. They have an opportunity to break through to their humility, their honest feelings, their courage, their self-honesty and integrity. Often, at such times, people finally call out for help. Challenges can help us break through the crust so we can re-connect to our hearts and to our will and take responsibility for the moment.

The gift in each challenging event in our lives is that it can re-connect us to our own hearts and to the hearts of others. Extraordinary events can do so extraordinarily, if we let them.

They wake us up and can free us from the pile of stuff we have let accumulate around us and around our hearts, letting in the light of feeling and aliveness.

The gift of the heart 'in the matter,' the gift at the core of each challenging opportunity, is that it can reconnect us to our own hearts, by helping us break through the stuff we have allowed to cover who we truly are.

What mattered to me

I remember a time many years ago, when I took an active role in maintaining a meditation center. For the most part, people came to the center in order to support their own meditation practice. However, from time to time, a person would come with other agendas. When that happened, I felt it was my responsibility to intervene, and to protect the interests of the people that came to deepen their meditation.

Ironically, in those days, I was very quick to take care of others, and very slow to take care of myself. I tried to treat everyone fairly, even when they acted unfairly against me. That stance was pushed to the limit when a very shrewd and manipulative operator entered the picture. He sought my position, and he saw me as someone that stood in the way of his influence. He also clearly saw my weakness: I did not act out of my own self interests, and he knew that my stance would eventually leave me depleted, unsupported and isolated. Time was on his side. All he had to do was actively engage in strengthening his own influence and work against mine.

Believe it or not, it took several years before the crust around my heart finally developed cracks. I was stubborn, and I had a powerful ego playing the role of a nice guy. Therefore, I endured a lot of pounding, a lot of negative experiences. Eventually, I got sick. I developed arthritis followed by a life threatening swelling around my heart. That's what it took to wake me up!

What this finally revealed to me, was that I was taking care of everyone but myself. I was taking myself for granted, and even the people that I thought I was helping were taking me for granted. I had been living in a delusion that I was doing the right thing. I was ignoring the most important thing — respecting my own life. I had not been defending myself or taking care of myself. Instead, I was defending everything else. I was defending my crust, and this crust had literally grown as a life threatening physical swelling around my own heart!

In time and with little choice, I learned to give up my false role and to take care of my feelings. In that shift from protecting my false sense of who I was, from what 'mattered' to me to what mattered for being in my heart, I finally began to learn how to own my power and take responsibility for myself and my purpose. Ironically, it was that shift that brought my spiritual journey back on track. And as I shifted to being centered, my illness evaporated. I healed.

If I had not suffered, I would more than likely be wasting away in that ignorance of playing the role of a nice guy for others, but not for my self. And, I would be continuing to take care of my crust, surrounding myself with the pain that came from holding false identifications of who I am. The gift, the heart of the matter for me, was rediscovering myself, my purpose and my own aliveness. That gift saved my life.

What mattered to Bill

A long time ago, my friend Bill, was a department head responsible for coordinating and directing a prestigious medical research team. He worked long hours, never taking any time off, sacrificing family time and pretty well everything else, because he knew that people's hopes for cures and perhaps their very lives depended on him.

Exhausted, after a number of years, he developed pneumonia. He was hospitalized. His recovery, because of his exhaustion and other complications, took weeks. Understandably, he was nervous and concerned about what his absence would do to all of the research he had been supervising. Later, he was shocked to find out that everyone did much better in his absence!

His colleagues' success during his absence forced him to

realize how controlling he had been. There were many competent people who could easily take on most of the responsibilities, in some cases better than he could. In fact, his obsession with being present and taking everything on had gotten in the way. This episode was pivotal for Bill. He learned to let go, to relax, to trust and to have faith. His health improved. He was happier. He spent much more time with family and friends. And people began to appreciate him more in his work.

The crisis that Bill underwent broke through some of the crust that had accumulated around his sense of who he was. He had acted from that crust by being overly controlling, hard on others and on himself. When he finally relaxed and let go of much of what he was carrying, he was freed to be closer to his heart, to who he really was. He also became much more effective in all areas of his life.

Bill underwent a life transformation that was sparked by an illness. Sometimes, we postpone our transformations, our chances to break the crust around our hearts until it threatens our very existence. Yet, why wait until you have a heart attack to make the changes and become alive again? Unfortunately, too many people do wait.

What matters to you?

More often than not, life tends to send out all kinds of messages when you are not acting from your heart or from your own best interests because you are holding on to the very things that keep you out of your heart. Unfortunately, rather than listening, we tend to try harder.

Where do you tend to get caught? Do you know the warning signs of being pulled away from your heart and into what seems to matter more than being fully alive? Are you willing to heed theses signs and reevaluate your responsibility to yourself, or do you want to wait until the pressure builds?

Here are some warning signs that you may be overextended in supporting your crust:

1. **Your energy decreases.** Often, because you are disconnected from your heart and joy, there is less vitality in the way you interact with the world. That drop in energy can signal to you that something that you are holding on to has wedged itself between your heart and actions.

2. **Your enthusiasm decreases.** Have you stopped waking up looking forward to your day? Is your day filled with obligations and 'shoulds' rather than a feeling of excitement, eagerness and cheerfulness?

3. **Your self worth decreases.** When you are not looking after your own best interests, you are letting your own system know that other things or other people are more important than you.

4. **Your time for yourself decreases.** If you become caught up in something that begins to consume you, it also begins to consume your time for yourself, your own happiness, play and joy.

5. **You begin to blame others.** If you are not taking responsibility for your own feelings and for being caught in your own issues, the tendency is to blame others, especially others that do not agree with you.

6. **You ignore people trying to help you.** Because you are caught up in your own issues, you are likely defensive and protective of what is in that crust, and are more than likely to interpret help as interference.

7. **You resist asking for help.** Has tunnel vision set in? Has your ego blinded you to the fact that you may be way off course? Do you feel like you can do everything yourself?

8. **You feel that you have a cause.** Has your sense of worth become entangled in what you are doing? Have you confused

taking responsibility of something outside of yourself with taking responsibility for yourself?

9. **You stopped growing.** Does it seem as if you are not moving forward in your life or in your career, and you can't quite figure out what is going on? Perhaps it is the crust you are feeding that is growing, instead of you.

There is always a lesson and a gift in things that turn out differently than the way we want the universe to unfold. Otherwise, we would experience a universe that was boxed in with all of our issues, avoidances, defensiveness and fears. It would be devoid of presence, of life. It would just be our crust.

Often, when we try to hold on to our crust and to the things that we believe matter, we want the world to change. In a way, we want to contract the world, the things and the people around us, so that we can be comfortable holding our identification to our wounds and to what matters to us.

It doesn't work that way. The world is bigger than we are. In order to be fully in the world, we ourselves have to become bigger. We need to create the space to become more open to what the world has to offer. To help us create that space, we need to let go of the crust, the attachment to things we think matter, when they really don't.

We have to do this, or the universe will do it for us. When the universe does begin to do it for us, we need to recognize the gift, the heart in the matter.

We are all faced with great opportunities... brilliantly disguised as impossible situations.

Author Unknown

Chapter Summary

In this chapter, we looked at how our hurts, avoidances and attachments begin to define us to the point of becoming what matters to us, out of proportion to their value in our lives. Often, the gift in the obstacles and challenges is their ability to help us break away the false identification, and the crust, revealing our aliveness and vitality

The Mind and the Heart

Do you know where your mind is?

This chapter takes another look at feelings and emotions, but this time from the perspective of the mind.

Finding the mind

We are all familiar with the mind as the part of us that thinks! Most of us, if asked where the mind is, would point to our heads. Where else would it be? Believe it or not, the natural resting place of the mind is in the heart. Surprised or not convinced?

The heart is free, and through our heart, feelings arise freely, spontaneously. That spontaneity can extend to our mind, our thoughts and intentions. When the mind is centered, unperturbed and relaxed, it naturally settles here. In the heart, the mind can be open to the moment, to the experience of joy, to a sense of fullness and delight. These are actually the experiences we crave, and we often spend large amounts of money on vacations and entertainment to achieve even a glimpse of them.

Many of the practices in the great spiritual traditions prepare the mind to settle in the heart. Practices, such as prayer, meditation, and contemplation, chanting and even selfless or voluntary service tend to clear the mind of the negative impressions and experiences we tend to hold on to, and free it to re-enter the present moment of the heart.

People who act from their heart, and with their minds centered there, often have a power of presence that is contagious, attracting and effective. Part of the reason that we are attracted to such people, is that simply being in their presence encourages us to also come closer to our hearts and to our own joy.

Forgetting our heart

We live in a culture that to a large extent denies being in the heart. Consider how we greet people as they are walking by. We may ask each other how we are doing, yet the tendency is to lie – to say that we are doing fine, when some of the time, this is not the case. Often, we are not even aware of the other's stance or their body language. If we paid more attention to their body language, we might observe the contradiction between what is said and what is felt.

Instead of noticing this contradiction, we tend to focus on the upper body, especially the head and eyes. There is often complicity in the process, since both people are putting up a mask, a front. It is a public face that is showing, and both people accept and to some extent support each other's act. It is a kind of socially accepted pre-agreement not to pry, not to uncover the ruse.

In our culture, expressing how we feel is to some extent frowned upon. Denying how we feel is often looked upon as a sign of strength. What tends to be acknowledged is logical thought, rational action, and coolness under fire, level-headedness, politeness and conviction. To some extent, under pressure to belong, we learn to act from our heads, and disconnect from our hearts. Feelings and their expression may be seen as a liability.

This stance, however, creates real problems. Ignoring our feelings actually works against our well-being, and in the end, puts us in a real disadvantage with others. Why? Because, in detaching ourselves from our feelings, we are also detaching ourselves from our freedom of being open to what the moment brings. It moves us away from our ability to think 'out of the box' and from freely experiencing joy.

In detaching ourselves from our feelings, we also tend to let go of our power and presence. People who are in touch with their feelings, who do not hide from what they feel and can take care of their feelings appropriately, are often the ones who can sway people over to their direction, who are listened to and heard when they speak, whose words have more power and affect.

The flight from our heart to our head

Why do we retreat into our heads? Why do some of us end up thinking, justifying and analyzing as a means to avoid feeling? And then, why do we tend to remain in our heads and avoid returning to our hearts?

Let's take a look at how this process happens, so that we can better understand what is involved and so that we can do something about it.

The escape from the heart.

The natural resting place for the mind is in the heart. In this way, our mind basks in the freedom, spontaneity and courage of the heart. It is in part, the courage of the heart that gives us the freedom to have new ideas and to be willing to let go of ideas that no longer serve us.

When we are in our hearts and experience a shock, we lose that connection and our awareness of that shock clusters around the heart. We may experience this clustering around the heart as a heart ache. Part of that shock may move down to the area of the solar plexus, where we experience a 'knot,' a sense of a blow to the stomach, weakness, tension or pain.

Another part of that shock may move upwards towards the head, and towards objectivity, analyzing and even denial. The first significant passage on the way to the head is through the area of the throat.

Passage through our throat center

As the experience of shock and disconnection from the heart moves upwards through the neck, it manifests as a contraction of the normal functioning of the throat. We are all familiar with what happens here: the tightness, the dryness, the loss of timber and power in the voice. There may be difficulty in being clear or assertive with our voice and the right words may not appear. People may literally experience their words stuck in their throat. It is also here that we experience a contraction of our creativity, playfulness and self-expression. We may be aware of putting ourselves down with inner dialogue and negative self concepts.

The throat area is often referred to as the throat center or chakra, the subtle energy center that relates to speech, creativity and will. As our wave of contraction, in response to a shock or negative experience, leaves the area of the heart and moves upwards through the throat, these abilities become contracted in our throat center. Here, we also experience a contraction in our spontaneity, playfulness and self-expression. This contraction may also manifest as self deprecating inner dialogue and negative self concepts.

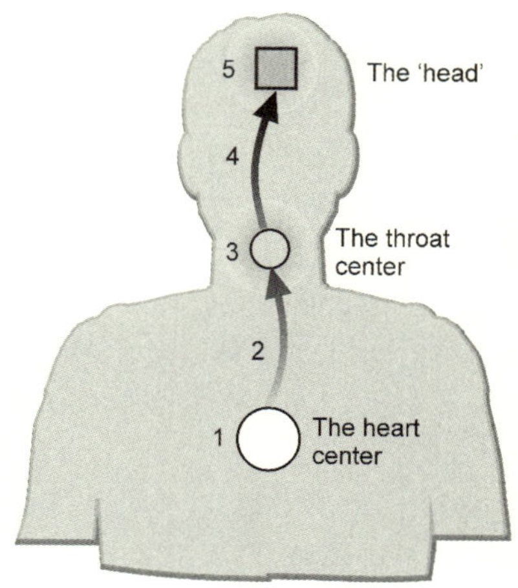

1. The natural resting place of the mind is in the spontaneity of the heart
2. When out of touch with our feelings, we may retreat in the direction of the head
3. Retreating from the heart, we tend to give away our will, value and creativity at the level of the throat center.
4. Retreating past the throat center, at the level of the eyes, we experience 'tunnel vision'
5. Disconnected from the heart, and having given away will, the mind tries to reconnect by analyzing and returning to the issues, which have now become emotions.

When our feelings get hurt, the tendency is to retreat into our head.

Giving away will

At the area of the throat, we experience the giving away of our will through our words, communication and actions, especially towards those that we perceive as the cause of our pain or contraction.

Why would we give away our will? As mentioned previously, the process starts when we feel disconnected from our core at the level of the heart. It is from our will that we responded. Our will tries to overcome the disconnection and bring us back to our hearts. We may be angry, disappointed or frustrated. When none of these actions re-connect us to our hearts, we try to elicit help from the people with whom we got hurt. We may demonstrate and express how we feel and seek their response. When this fails, we make the other person responsible for the shock that we experienced. In this way, we hold the hurt or wound, but give someone else the responsibility to do something about it, in order for us to heal. In making them responsible, we give away our will. Unfortunately, we need our will to heal.

Burning the bridge

In the process of giving away our will to others, we come to a very important crossroads. We can see our situation as the consequence of simply being out of touch with feeling and our heart, and, we can choose to make an effort to return to being centered in our feelings and in our heart. For example, if we are in the middle of an argument, we could just stop and go for a walk and 'cool off' or contemplate where we are, what happened and what we need. Often at this point, we can return to being centered, heal through our own efforts and return without anger or emotions. In this way, we also get our will and power back, through our own efforts.

On the other hand, we may continue to engage others or choose to stay in conflict instead of making our own effort to return to being centered. In the process, we risk making someone else responsible for how we feel. We give away responsibility for our will and place ourselves at the mercy or power of others, by waiting for them to change, to say they are sorry or that we are right. Essentially, we are burning the connecting bridge back to our own heart when we give our will away to others, and blame someone else for the damage.

Giving away power

When we burn that connecting bridge to being centered and in our heart, the people or situations we deem to be the cause become our center. They become the focus we seek, and later wait for in order to find resolution. In this way, we give away our power to someone else. We wait for them to say that they are sorry or we hold a grudge. We identify our experience with powerlessness and avoidance and fear, and this makes us even more susceptible to getting hurt the next time.

The habit of giving our power away is an extension of what we did as children. We learned to seek being taken care of by our parents and to make them responsible for helping us heal. Now as adults, we may be asking other people in our lives to continue taking on that parental role. We continue making them responsible for our hurt and disconnection from our heart. We continue giving them the power to turn things around for us.

As children, we may not have had access to that many options or choices. Yet as adults, we can take our power back, by reclaiming our responsibility, and by reclaiming our will to care for our feelings and needs, instead of making others responsible.

Contracting our sense of worth

The throat area is also associated with our sense of worth and valuing. The process of contracting away from the heart and moving toward the head, also signifies loss of value in relationship. We can experience that loss in our relationship with others and in our relationship and connection to feeling in the heart. This experience of loss is partly what fuels emotion, and reinforces blame. By giving away our will to others, we give away our validity, and make others responsible for our value.

Contracting our vision

Have you ever experienced the sense of tunnel vision when

you are under stress or running out of time to meet a deadline? In a similar way, our vision contracts as the shock of separation from the heart moves past our throat and through the vision centre, behind our eyes. This area is associated with how we create our sense of the world, its possibilities and limitations. As we experience contraction here, our sense of possibilities and fruitful outcomes decreases. The world loses some of its luster, color and brightness. We may become pessimistic. We may see things as fated, and our concepts and expectations may take on a sense of being grey, or even black and white.

Home alone

After passing the level of the throat, and after having given away our will, our mind then settles in the head. We have common expressions indicating this. People speak of someone being 'in their head', 'being all mental' or 'up in their own ivory tower.'

Being in our head in this way is much like someone who got thrown out of their home during a divorce. The way they got there becomes a major focus of their energy. The excuses, justifications and judgments begin to fill their thinking.

Without the will to bring us back to the heart, our emotional baggage and impressions begin to act as if they have a will of their own. As a result, we inundate our heads with negative commercials which reinforce the choices that resulted in our difficulties. Here, the painful and not integrated experiences may be recreated and replayed over and over again. Messages and impressions such as "*they*" are to blame, "*they*" need to say they are sorry, and "*poor little me!*" can echo unabated if we let them. We are quite capable of spending hours analyzing and sorting all of the details that got us into this mess, without doing much about it.

The hook of emotion and analyzing

The rift or separation from our hearts that landed us in our heads is painfully experienced, and maintained, at the level of emotion. In fact, one way of looking at emotions is as a way to hold the experience of separation from our feelings. Feelings are experienced in the moment, in our hearts. Emotions are what happen to our experiences when we do not let our selves feel and reconnect, when there is separation from heart and will.

Since emotions are the experiences of separation or contraction, it does very little good to immerse ourselves in them. In fact, the more we indulge in them, the more our sense of separation is increased. Thinking about what happened and going over it, also tends to increase more thinking and going over it, pulling emotion along with it. The added focus, time and energy we give to our experiences of separation increase the negative charge we store in our recollections and in our memories. As we store the experience of rejection strongly, it is more readily available to link to future experiences.

Why some counseling sessions, which focus solely on talking, get stuck or take too long to manifest change, is because the process of only focusing on thoughts, emotions, memories, events, dreams, etc., tends to keep us stuck in our heads. It is a lot like adding fuel to a fire in the hope of putting it out. It doesn't work that way. To get out of the trap, out of being stuck in the head, we need to find another way.

Following the path back to the heart

The path back to the heart lies in the choice of reversing the process that landed us in our heads, and separated us from our feelings in the first place. It is a process of undoing the damage, so that we can re-connect.

Step 1: Let go of hiding in your head

To begin this journey home, we must give up on solving our dilemma through analyzing or thinking our way out. We need to appreciate that as long as our mind is stuck in our head and disconnected from our heart, we are more likely to spin our wheels by going back over what has already happened.

For the most part, this simply reinforces the problem and interferes with taking the steps to move forward. Going back to the past rarely helps you move into the present moment. Instead, it is a well worn trap. Do not forget that the mind also needs to be rescued from being trapped in the head, away from the freedom of the heart. In fact, it is the heart than must rescue the mind.

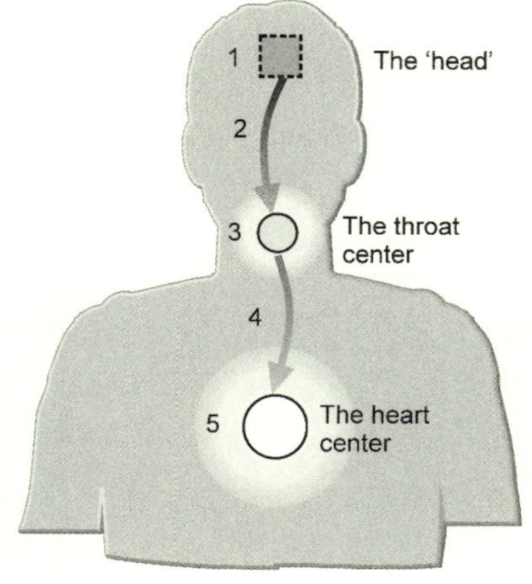

1. As we begin to pay attention to how we feel, we can take steps that free us from the trap of analyzing, going over old issues and getting stuck in emotions.
2. As we replace and let go of negative concepts of ourselves, we begin to see more opportunities.
3. Through demonstrating our worth and our will through actions, we regain our responsibility and trust for what we feel.
4. The courage to feel, act for ourselves and express our feelings pulls us to our hearts.
5. The mind returns to the spontaneity of the heart.

Taking care of your feelings and reconnecting with your heart

Step 2: Your intention to heal

You must turn things around by putting your focus in the direction of your heart. You must bring forth your intention to heal. Intention is very powerful. Intention is like aiming an arrow at a target. You must perform the action with your will in order to make the intention work. You have to pull the bow back and be willing to release it, so that your intention can reach its goal, and that goal is to return to your center.

Step 3: Take back your will

You have to take your will back. You have to take it back where you lost it; when you made others responsible for what happened to you. In the end, you are the only one responsible for what happened to you, because you are the one that experienced it, felt it and was stuck with the results! Most of us try really hard to fault others making them responsible for our problems. We try to shrink away from being present, from owning the whole of our experience, and thus, we end up diminishing ourselves.

We take back our will by doing action, by pulling back the bow, so to speak. By releasing the bow, by letting go of our dependence on others taking responsibility for our lives and our situations, we take back our will.

Step 4: Forgive yourself

You need to forgive yourselves for giving away your power. You gave away your power by making someone else responsible. Now, you have to take back that responsibility. You need to go right back to where you gave it away. Someone else didn't take it away. You gave it away. To bring it back, you need to acknowledge what you did, own it and forgive yourselves for having done that. It is about self-acceptance of your power. If you can forgive yourself, then you can demonstrate to yourself that you have the power to take back your joy.

Step 5: Take responsibility for your feelings now

The will needs to be harnessed to re-connect ourselves back to our heart. The will needs to be demonstrated by you taking care of your feelings and your heart. When you take appropriate actions to care for your feelings, especially around other people, you begin to trust and feel safe to return to your heart. It is fear that separates you from your heart; you got hurt before, and you don't want to get hurt again.

As you begin to take care of your feelings with others, you send a great message to the part of you that feels, "It is now safe to trust, to be alive, to feel and to express." Somebody is taking responsibility, someone is taking care of you, and that somebody is you.

Step 6: Own your worth and demonstrate your value to others

As you take care of your own best interests around others, you demonstrate your self worth to yourself and to others. This valuing pulls you to your heart and your feelings. As your own sense of worth and value rise, others sense it. People will respond to you in ways that will make it easier for you to be yourself, to play, to express, ask for what you need and to be open to receiving what they have to offer.

One of the by-products of this process is that the voice begins to become fuller, stronger, more resonant and more relaxed. This parallels the relaxing of the mind towards the heart at the level of the throat chakra, the subtle energy center related to speech, creativity and valuing.

Step 7: Stay in your heart

Take action so that you are less likely to be pulled away from your heart again. One of the simplest yet effective actions is to become aware of your breath. Breathing is very powerful as it affects the mind and thinking almost immediately. This is one reason why meditators focus the breath. It is why people are encouraged to take a deep breath before speaking in public. Breathing can relax you, ground you and center you, can help you resisting being pulled away from your heart and it can help you notice what is happening with your energy and feelings. As you breathe, you might want to visualize your breath feeding the flame in your heart, that spontaneous and joyful flame shining with courage and joy.

Using your mind to take care of your heart

Here is a short list to help you zero in on your feelings. Take the time to write down your answers as they pertain to a particular situation or issue in your life. Begin keeping a diary as it is a powerful tool for remembering, integrating and checking whether you are applying the potential of your observations into actions that help you transform.

- What are you feeling in the moment?
- Are you sad, disillusioned, scared, disappointed or angry?
- What do you want?

- What emotions are you bringing from your past?
- Can you set aside the drama that you may be wrapped in, and simply observe what you are actually feeling and wanting?
- If you could have cared for your feelings earlier, what would you have done differently?
- Should you have walked away?
- Were there other ways to protect yourself or take care of your feelings?
- What did you learn about yourself?
- Did you learn something you could use in a positive way at a later date?
- Are you willing to forgive yourself for taking the stance or punishment that you took?
- Are you willing to accept yourself along with the faults that may have been revealed?

Putting your will back to work

All of these questions can point the mind and will in the right direction. However, the next step is actually doing something about it! You have to exercise your will, in order to own it, to take it back after giving it away through blame or holding the stance of being the victim. You have to begin training your mind to notice your feelings, in real time.

For some people, it takes time for them to notice what they felt or wanted or even needed to say. Sometimes, there can even be a delay of hours between the time an incident occurred and the time they finally realize what they felt, wanted, and needed to do. Even in such cases, with patience and effort, the time lag can be reduced to minutes, then seconds. It is very important to notice and be aware of your feelings, as you are feeling them. Therefore, make a true effort to discern, to pause if necessary and to reflect on the events happening around you.

A diary serves as a very good tool to, at the end of the day, jot down what happened, what you did, what you learned, and what you need to remember to do next time. You might consider asking a good and trusted friend to be your coach in the process of getting past bad habits. Compare notes as to what occurred, yet be prepared to be non-judgmental, and don't get caught in analyzing what happened — your job is to use your resources to help you move forward.

You may find that you need to actually practice noticing and protecting your feelings. In this case, start out with things that don't tend to carry a charge for you. Take care of your feelings by noticing them, acknowledging them and then finding an appropriate action.

If someone seeks you out in order to share their negative experiences and basically dump on you, you need to be responsible enough with your feelings to be able to either walk away, find an excuse to walk away, tell them that it is not the right time, or simply say, "I really can't hear this right now." You can choose to be polite, yet you must choose to be firm. You must choose to demonstrate both to yourself and to others, that you are willing to take care of your feelings, that you walk your talk, that you walk with your heart.

Look over what you have observed and written down in your diary. Determine what you need to do to take care of your feelings and your heart. Start practicing. In order to build up your confidence and trust in yourself, begin with what is less threatening and easier to do. Each time you put your will to work, you'll be a step closer to the real you.

The consequence of taking care of your feelings

As has already been mentioned, we are attracted to others who act from their hearts. When we begin to look after our own hearts, by noticing and then appropriately protecting and nurturing our own feelings, we are subtly letting our whole energetic system know that it is safer to be in-the-moment, safer to feel more, relax more, and allow more of ourselves out into the world. Once we begin to establish ourselves from the heart, from the truth of our feelings, we are drawn into a richer experience of the present moment.

When the mind rests in the heart

What is it like to have our minds rest in our hearts? What is it like not to be constantly harassed by ideas and worries about the past or future. What is it like not having the pressure to think or do all of the time?

Take a look at people who are in this state all or most of the time. How did Mother Teresa behave around others? How does the Dhali Lama respond to questions? When we look at the behavior of saints and ecstatic beings, we notice that they are very free. They are very open to the present moment. There is a profound simplicity, uncomplicated by the emotional garbage that most of us carry. In some ways, they are like infants or young children. Their eyes blaze with the openness to receive and to share. They are very present, very receptive to the moment, to what life has to offer. In fact, their presence can be disarming. There is no push. They just are, being, very much themselves.

It is not enough to make these beings responsible for holding the ideal of a mind resting in the heart. It is not enough that they are just our heroes. It is not enough that they hold the possibility of what we could be, while we go on with our lives. Although they show to us what is possible, you must experience that state for yourself.

Begin by taking the hints and suggestions in this chapter and in the rest of the book to heart. Make the shifts and choices that bring you closer to being in your heart. Every moment that you are not in your heart is a waste of time. Stop wasting your time. Start making the choices that bring you to being alive. What is it like to have your mind in your heart? Find out by doing, and you will know.

Being in the heart is a very easy and natural state. What keeps us from being there all or most of the time, is that we have developed habits of being somewhere else. Start working on your habits and choices. Let go of the ones that don't work for you. Be centered and positively contagious!

Chapter Summary

In this chapter, we looked at the journey our mind takes when we experience separation from the heart. That journey involves giving away to others our will, our sense of value and our power. We often end up trying to regain the situation from a perspective that seeks objectivity and analysis in order to reconnect to what was lost. This, however, maintains separation from the heart.

The journey back to the heart requires that we re-engage our will, our sense of worth and our power, through actions that take care of our feelings and demonstrate our will and worth to ourselves and to others.

Part 3
Regaining Your Center

Regaining Your Power

Your own Healing Journey

Owning your power

When children express their joy, enthusiasm and aliveness, they are manifesting their own personal power. Your power lies in that same ability to manifest who you are, to express your intentions and will. Your expression of your own power is not different from your experience of joy, because power comes from feeling and from the heart.

When we do not own our power, when we stop acting from our hearts, we disconnect from power; this is where power gets its negative associations. Disowned power is applied out of fear and reaction. We experience disowned power as force used against us, or as abuse, drama, manipulation and ruthlessness. Power used in these ways lacks compassion and joy, and it is false because it is reactive and superficial.

True power is transformative. It comes from a deep place within you, and connects you to that same deep place. True power reveals your greatness. When you own your power, are true to yourself and can act from your heart, you have access to your greatness.

When power is disowned

Children can experience the intensity of disowned power from their parents and care givers. There may have been heated family arguments in the home over money and relationship issues; there may have been threats of force, drama and intensity that overwhelmed and de-centered the children. Witnessing disowned power or being its target, can leave painful impressions and emotional scars.

Children tend to be very ego-centric. When they experience power being used in a negative way, especially towards them, they perceive that something is wrong with them, that they are the cause of the abuse of power and they are to blame. They take responsibility for the actions of the parents and try to be 'good,' 'perfect,' pure and spotless, in order to remove themselves from being the problem or cause. In order to achieve this, power is disowned and purged from the system. What develops is a sense that power is dark, bad, mean and not good to have.

Often, there is great sensitivity in the hurt that follows the abuse of power. That sensitivity can express itself in the decision to never use power against anyone else, to never hurt anyone else the same way.

That sensitivity also expresses itself as the taking care of others. We can feel another person's pain. We take care of others the way we would have wished someone would have taken care of us.

The irony is that in taking care of others in this way, we often ignore our own best interests. We 'mother' others, instead of ourselves. We are pulled to help others and offer our energy. Meanwhile, we are not getting what we need, and get drained in the process.

Sometimes, simply accepting our power can be so uncomfortable that we hold it back, deny it or give it away to others, either consciously or unconsciously. With this can come a stance of being 'nice' and non-threatening to others. People actually seek encouragement and approval from others for taking this powerless stance.

Approval from others will never replace what is lost and being given away. When you disown your power, you are actually rejecting a part of your true self, who you really are, a part of your very being. When you disown your power you disown your intensity, passion and joy.

Symptoms of giving power away

One of the clearest symptoms that you have given away your power is that people tend to dump their negative issues on you; their stories, negative emotions, experiences, frustrations or sense of burden. You know you have been dumped on because you feel energetically worse afterwards.

Why do you get dumped on? You have rejected or given away your own power in some way. This loss of power manifests as a weakening in your energy or energetic field. Now, the very people you need to avoid seek you out, because they can sense from a distance that you are an easy target. They can sense that they can discard some of their negative charge onto you, and your weakened will, and avoidance of using your own power, makes it safe for them to do so. They can count on your sympathy.

I have observed, in some people, the tendency to steal energy from others. They do this in a number of ways, primarily by trying to grab attention from people in a good, yet open state, or, they try to get rid of their own negative energy or feelings by sharing it with others.

Does the concept seem a bit off the wall to you? We do have expressions such as "*He was a pain in the neck*," or "*I found her to be a real downer.*" Often, these people have difficulty holding their own energy, so they hang around people that give them attention. Think about the times you felt drained after talking to someone.

Although most theft of energy is through attention, sharing and sympathy, some people have learned to grab at the more subtle energy people carry in their state, feelings and enthusiasm. If you ever watch closely the interactions of people at a party or any social event, watch what people do with their hands, because that is often how this kind of energy is accessed.

I once witnessed a rather extreme example of an energy thief in the form of a middle aged woman who entered and walked down the aisle of a bus. She managed to place her hand on most of the people she passed by. I remember noticing her game plan, and pulled myself out of her reach. After passing me, she actually returned, reached for my shoulder, and literally said, "*I guess I missed you*!" It was a blatant attempt to steal the energy of well-being that we all carry, and she knew it. What allowed her to get away with this, is that most people either didn't notice her intent, or more sadly, had become conditioned to this kind of theft as a matter of course!

In order not to give away your well being and power, you have to learn to keep them centered on your own heart. Otherwise, they may scatter to the whims and needs of others. It is most important to own your power.

Noticing

How do you begin to own your power? It is important to begin noticing when you give your power away. For example, do you tend to automatically take care of another person's feelings, at a detriment to yourself? Do you habitually choose a position with a group of people that diminishes your effectiveness? Do you notice in speaking to others, you have a habit of putting yourself down, or speak too quietly? Do you seek support or approval from others rather than use the time to convince them to follow your lead? Do you feed others your ideas and effort, and then end up being unacknowledged for what you have given?

Patterns of giving power away can sometimes be so ingrained, it may take some effort to reveal them. Keeping a journal and jotting down some possible instances is one way to begin the process of noticing when you are giving away your power. Often it occurs when you ignore your own feelings as you interact with others. To help you discern when these instances occur, try applying this short query:

- When does my energy drops around other people?
- When do I back away from what I intend to say or do?
- When do I not take care of my feelings?
- When do I take care of other's feelings or sensitivities, but ignore my own?
- At meetings and in social interactions, do I choose to place myself in the weak or powerless locations?
- Do people tend to ignore me when I have something to say? When this happens, do I allow it?
- When confronted by others, does it take me too long to know how I am feeling? Does the delay in my response result in failing to act decisively in the moment?

If at first you have difficulty discerning your feelings, focus on your energy levels, and focus on how your energy rises or falls during different situations with people. If you summarize your day in your journal, take time to note what would have been better strategies to use next time. The important thing is to notice and acknowledge when you give away power, so that you can begin to take responsibility for it.

Forgiveness is welcoming back your power

Forgiveness is a means of regaining your connection with your heart, and letting go of the influences that block that connection. This is the root of 'for-giveness'. Before you can give, or act appropriately, you have to go to the place from which true giving and action arise, and this place is your own heart.

You gave away your responsibility for owning your power. You can't regain it by continuing to make others responsible to give it back. You can only get your power back by returning to the original responsibility of owning it. In owning that responsibility, you have to forgive yourself for having given your power away in the first place. In this way, you take back your own responsibility and power by no longer making others responsible for your own process. You are taking back your will. You are returning to being your own center of action.

How to regain your power

Regaining your power actually follows the reverse process to how it was lost, given away or denied. **It is important to understand that you never actually lose your power, and can never really give it away. What you give away is your responsibility for using your power, your responsibility to derive benefit from it, or your responsibility to experience the joy of being in your power.** Even feeling powerless is an active process, for it actually takes energy and constant vigilance to maintain your sense of powerlessness. If you relax, even for a short time, your power would surely begin to seep back into your being!

So the question of how to get your power back is really a question about how to stop sabotaging power. The primary way of sabotaging power is identifying power as a bad part of ourselves, and banishing it from the identification of who we are. This is not something we do just once. We repeatedly push our power away, or continually give it away to others, in order not to feel that we are 'bad'. This pushing away takes time and energy and thus can manifest as a loss of energy and enthusiasm.

What would happen if you stopped pushing away your power? What would happen if instead of blaming someone else when you give away your power, or waiting for them to change, you decided to tell yourself that you are sorry for letting go of your power? What would happen if you forgave yourself for initially and repeatedly giving away your power? You might be surprised! You might find out that your power never left! You might find out that all that was going on was that you were simply not owning it and pushing it away!

The shamanic journey

The re-connection to our own power, joy and healing is expressed in native traditions as a healing journey of transformation, in fact, a shamanic journey. Although the details of this journey vary from one part of the world to another, the main elements remain the same. A village elder, shaman or spiritual advisor initiates you and prepares you for your journey. Sometimes, it is a dream or vision that starts the process. As a seeker, you then set out on a journey to leave your tribe, village, family or friends and venture into the greater unknown. That unknown can take the form of the forest, the desert, the mountain or a cave. What is left behind are all of the conditionings, socializations, attachments, cues, reinforcements, obligations and hooks to an earlier way of being. You enter the greater unknown with the courage of your conviction and heart. The intention is clear — to regain power and wholeness. As the seeker, you are asked to be open to your dreams, to the inner guidance, to trust the process and to have faith in the outcome.

During this journey, many of the habits of giving away power have already been left behind with family and friends. Now, new situations and experiences bring face-to-face encounters with the present moment, with your senses and true feelings. In a way, you are thrust into confronting the experience of the world in a manner that is closer to the experience of a child: primal, new, and immediate. You experience a way of being in the world not separated from your power, before power was given away.

It is not so much about finding power, as it is about re-connecting with it and losing the tendencies which hold it back. This journey of faith, and trust in your own self and in the universe, opens up the heart. You face the tendencies and fears that keep your power away. Eventually, your own power is gifted back to you. It is the gift of the journey, of the universe and of your intention, your will and love for yourself and for the universe.

You return to your roots and tribe, a different person. You now own your power and a deep connection within yourself and with the world. It is from this deep connection that the shaman draws and expresses his or her power, and a healer can heal. Having made this journey in real life, having re-connected to power, the shaman becomes a catalyst for others to do the same. By embodying that power, the shaman's own presence encourages others to make the same journey, the same reconnection.

Your own shamanic journey

A shamanic journey may seem out of context to your present situation, but in essence, you can make a similar journey. You may need to take a series of smaller journeys, but eventually the destination is the same. The steps for your own journey start by letting go of the false belief that others hold your power, or that you have lost your power. If you still hold experiences that have convinced you of that, then these need to be revisited from a new stance; that of a warrior, of someone who learns to choose the courage of their own heart. Are you ready to start this journey?

Know that each experience you hold as one of having 'lost' power, it was you that gave it away. Therefore, it is you that must take power back! Take your power back. Learn to forgive yourself for having given your power away in the first place. In forgiving yourself, you acknowledge that it is your power and that it was your choice to give it away. Now it is still your choice, but you can choose to take back what is yours.

Observe your interactions with others, especially friends and family. Become aware of what you do with power, whom you give it to and who in turn takes it and why. What is your pattern of self-defeat? For many people, the pattern is to ignore their own feelings, their own best interests, and instead to take care of, feed, support, encourage or defend the needs of those around them. The ability to take care of your own feelings is often there, but it is used for everyone else. Now is the time to begin taking appropriate care of your own feelings, your own needs.

The consequence of accepting and taking care of your feelings is that you begin to trust it is safe to be in your feelings, it is safe to feel more joy, more aliveness, more enthusiasm and power. Please understand that I am not talking about emotions, I am talking about feelings, the free expression of your energy and state. Re-connecting with feeling is really about allowing yourself to return to a sense of wholeness, of being centered in your heart. Your feelings directly relate to your experience of being alive. Holding back your feelings, or not taking care of them, means cutting back on your aliveness, on your joy and your openness to what life has to offer. Opening yourself to your feelings, by acknowledging them and protecting them, opens you up to your joy, your humanness. Become more alive and each moment becomes richer, more real.

As you forgive yourself for originally rejecting your own power, you are in a position to welcome your power back into your life. You can take a caring and validating attitude towards your feelings, to your own heart. And that attitude can express itself in relation to others, in the actions you choose that care, nurture and protect your feelings. It is your attitude and your actions that actually take you across on this journey to reinstate your power.

Take each instance of taking care of your feelings and of successfully owning your power to be a journey. Know that each time you demonstrate to your inner child you are taking care of yourself, that action expands the trust of your whole being to be alive and powerful. Each time opens the door to power and joy and grace a little wider inside of your being. Each time transforms you. It is your journey.

The consequences of owning our power

One of the foremost consequences of owning your power is that you feel more joy and are more alive. For most people, suppressing their power means suppressing their feelings in general, and of course, the casualties are the joy and enthusiasm of being alive and looking forward to each day. All of this time, when you thought you were hiding from power, you may have been actually hiding from your own joy!

Another consequence of taking back your power is that your voice tends to become fuller, more resonant. As you speak, more people listen to what you have to say, because there is more feeling and power behind your words. Closely connected to your voice is your sense of worth. Taking back your power is a demonstration that you value yourself, and as a consequence, others respond to your new stance by valuing you back. Not only are you more open to being valued by others and to receive from them, but you also become more open to what the universe has to offer. You become more open to taking advantage of opportunities instead of sitting on the fence and letting your chances go past you.

Taking back your power also frees you from being the victim, as others are much less likely to dump their negativities on you. Instead, you are more likely to be a catalyst for these people. Having made the journey to regain your own power, you act as a real example of the possibilities available and encourage others.

By owning your power, others will treat you with more respect, partly because in re-accepting your feelings and power, you tend to let go of a lot of your fear. A posture of more power and less fear attracts people. Most people tend to follow, rather than lead, because they themselves are giving away power. When you own your power, you become a center around which people can gather. You yourself become a source of leadership and effectiveness.

Chapter Summary

In this chapter, we looked at the journey of our power, of the experiences that held our power back, and the process of regaining that power. We learned that we never actually lose our power. We lose our connection to our heart and our willingness to hold our joy and our sense of being powerful. The journey back to power is a journey of self-acceptance.

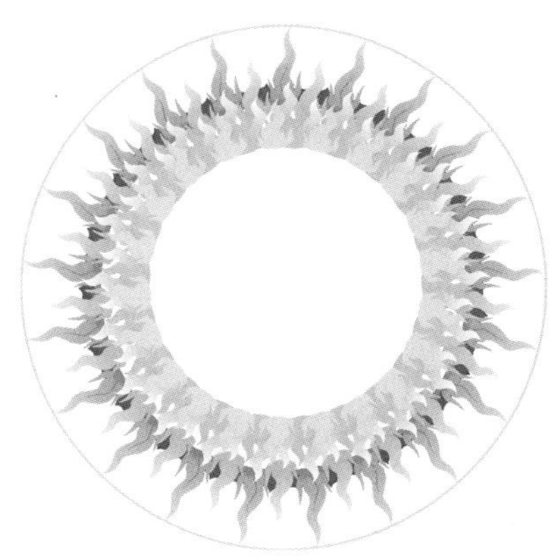

Will

Your will allows you to function in the world according to your intentions and in harmony with your feelings. Will tends to be associated with the throat area and the throat chakra. Along with will, this area of the throat is also associated with self worth and creativity. When you express your will, your voice is strong and resonant.

Do you know how will, self worth and creativity are related? They all come from being centered. You experience will in the heart, in the creative freedom of the moment. When you are in your heart, you have the freedom to express your will, your intentions, your value and your creative play.

There is, as well, an anatomical relationship between the will and the heart. The nerves that control the heart, lungs, arms and chest all originate in the neck, which as we have mentioned, is associated with will. In fact, the neck acts as a kind of coordinating center for much of our posture and expression. If you have ever watched a cat fall from a height, you will see he first orients his neck, and then place his body and feet towards the direction of landing. First the neck aligns, then the rest of the body. The neck defines how the head, posture and stance are held. For this reason, when people hold back their will, that holding manifests itself as a drooping head and body posture. In the same manner, when you re-connect to your core, activating and aligning your posture, you reveal a strong will.

What is will?

Will is your ability to affect your future, to make changes in the world around you and to take your intentions into action. When you say that you will do something, you are expressing your intention and ability to do so. You are also saying that it is done, that you will make it so.

Ultimately, will is what connects your own heart with actions. When your connection to your heart and feelings is clear and uncluttered, you act freely. You own your will.

Will and anger

When you get angry, it is the very same will that expresses itself as that anger. Your will is still trying to maintain your freedom of action and return you to connection with the heart. Your will is still trying to return to the experience of being in the flow of the moment, only now in anger, it is like a fish out of water.

If you watch a fish that is out of water, it will start thrashing and making every effort to express its shock and return to the water. It is frightened, and will try to defend itself if it can. For this reason, it can be dangerous to be around a larger fish that has teeth, barbs or stings.

If you return the fish back to the water, it will swim away. The fish is back in its element, back in its flow. It is alike our will disguised as anger. Once we have resolved our disconnection from our heart, or set things right, our will goes back to what it does best; it returns to acting for the continuity of our heart.

Just like a fish that has not returned back to the water, we are faced with a problem when our will and anger do not return us back to the heart. When all of our demonstrations and 'thrashing around' fail, when our immediate response do not remove our disconnection, we begin to retreat from the situation and from owning our will. We still seek agency, action and reconnection. However, when we give up on our own agency and responsibility to manifest the changes we seek, we begin to make others responsible and blame others.

At this point, our disowned will leads to emotion. Although our will is still there, it can not reconnect to the heart on its own. Disconnected from the heart, all will can do is thrash around. This is why, when our emotions are triggered, they seem to have a will of their own.

When people continue to be afraid to express their will, the will that hid in anger, begins to hide in rage. Each step of removing will from the freedom of the heart increases the degree to which will is disowned, until we quite literally lose our will. Therefore, if we do not want to lose our will, we have to make sure that we are acting from our hearts, from our feelings and freedom of being.

Will and intention

At one level, our will is what manifests our intention. It connects where we want to go with our ability to get there.

When we begin to trust our own power and our own process, and begin to let go of our tendencies to hold ourselves back, we begin to experience the effect of intention at a deeper level. This happens as we clear the hold of our negative beliefs about ourselves and what we are doing. As we begin to act more from the heart and in the flow of the moment, and less in our thinking, expectations and fears, we act without being reactive. Then, our will is strong and our intention is focused. Then, the hesitation and delay between intention and action is removed.

Ultimately, and taken to its extreme, the separation between will and intention decreases, until intention, will and action appear as one — a union of qualities by which we traditionally describe great beings and saints. A more easily recognized example occurs in the martial arts and in dance. By practicing under proper instruction, a dancer can achieve movement that is seemingly devoid of resistance or awkwardness. In this we see beauty. A true master of martial arts can move or resist great force, through manifesting their intention through their will.

How do we lose will?

We actually never lose our will. It is always present. What we can lose is our connection to our will.

In most situations where there has been a separation from feeling, from being fully present in the moment, there has also been a separation to some degree from will. This can happen as a result of a shock to our system, through a bad experience or a trauma. In these cases, we lose our connection to our heart, and when we can't reconnect, we end up with fear, emotion and disowned will.

When we try to direct our will, with that part of ourselves that reacts, contracts or tries to control out of fear, then the very expression of the will becomes contracted, and behaves as if was given away. This is because, will is being expressed by a part of us that is not centered, a part that has given away power.

To rescue our will, to find it again, we have to reach out with the part of us that is willing to reconnect to our heart and our power. And doing this, we validate our worth, our feelings and our being, and reestablish courage and freedom with our will.

Why is it so important to demonstrate will?

You demonstrate your will when you get things done. With will action speaks louder than words. It is through appropriate actions that your trust in yourself is strengthened. There are three important reasons why you need to demonstrate your will. Let's look at them more closely.

Demonstrating your will gets things done.

You connect to the world through actions and in turn you are affected by the actions of others. Without actions, it is difficult to manifest change.

Simply being aware of where you are stuck, or what

happened to you, rarely changes where you are stuck or what you hold. Having new insights allows you to make new or different choices. Yet, until you actually use your will to act on these new choices, very little changes. The material that you hold and identify with, is like the clutter in your closet. Having a different understanding of what the clutter represents, or even learning new ways of organizing this clutter, has little practical value until we decide and do something about the clutter. In that doing, will is applied. Until then, there is no demonstration of will, and little forward action.

Demonstrating your will strengthens trust in yourself.

As you apply your will, you prove to yourself that you are capable. Each time your will is tested and proven, it strengthens you. The actual performance of your actions in the world accumulates experiences of accomplishment, and successful strategies, for dealing with future situations. In this way, the will is much like your muscles - the more you use your will, the stronger you become and the more at-ease you become in expressing your will.

Demonstrating your will increases your willingness to trust.

First, you need to demonstrate that you are willing to take care of yourself. As a result, your will and actions help break through old beliefs, fears, past experiences of not being cared for and its consequences - a lack of trust in yourself and others. As you begin to take care of yourself, trust in yourself and in your ability to be an active and free agent in the world strengthens. You have demonstrated that you act in your own best interests. Your trust in yourself opens you to trust others and what the world has to offer.

How do we get our will back?

We get our will back by exercising it; the expression, 'Use it or lose it' applies. Often we develop bad habits in learning to hold back on our will and self-expression, or, we edit the expression of our will in response to others, because we seek rewards or might fear the consequences. By owning our will, by recognizing it as an expression of our own freedom and not as something to give away to others, we ourselves can reintroduce our own will into our lives.

Following are areas to look at, to help free your will:

Will recovery checklist – General Guidelines

- **Be observant of how you interact with others.** Do you stand by your truths? Do you protect what matters to you; your feelings and what you value? Do you have clear boundaries? Do you trust your self, or are you easily swayed to doubt yourself or your abilities in response to the stance of others? If you see that you have a tendency to give in, catch yourself and do something about it.

- **Catch yourself when you are being overly nice.** Choosing to hide behind a mask that is overly nice to others, creates internal conflict and damage, if at the same time, you are not being very nice to yourself; if you are lying about your true feelings and needs. It is very difficult to be that nice to everyone without holding back on the expression of your will. If you get into the habit of not expressing your will and not acting appropriately, you risk losing trust in yourself and, you risk surrounding yourself with people that will take advantage of your lack of will.

- **Free up your will.** Risk speaking your truth to others, through feelings rather than judgments. Interestingly, when we fear speaking our truth, we collect the very people around us that wish to suppress our truth, and, when we begin speaking our truth, we tend to gather around us people that encourage us.

- **Have discrimination.** Do not accept everything that someone says without testing its validity. Do not assume that everyone who is nice to you is your friend. Applying discrimination to your interaction with others maintains your freedom as a free agent, and protects your free will. The habits of being aware and discriminative, keep your will polished, active and ready to use.

- **Choose an instance where you gave away your will.** It is important to contemplate situations where you did not exercise your will. What would you do differently now? Are there still ongoing areas in your life where you are giving away too much ground, too much value, or not standing up for yourself, your feelings or what matters to you? Consider why you do it. What do you gain? What do you lose? It may be helpful to 'sit with it' for at least a few minutes. If necessary, seek the council or support of a close friend.

  After you have contemplated, write your thoughts in a diary or sheet of paper. Write down your observations as to what happened, how you felt and what you would do in a similar situation the next time it occurs. Be clear and realistic. Choose actions that are appropriate and not reactive.

- **Demonstrate your will.** Remember that when it comes to will, simply noticing or understanding why you do things is not enough. You actually need to demonstrate your will, both to yourself and to others, in order to affect change, in order to move forward. Follow through on your intentions. Take your will back and with it you take back your trust in your self and your ability to seek what is best for you.

- **Do something you avoid doing.** Most people when given a list of tasks to do, tend to start with what attracts them and leave to last what they avoid. Unfortunately, what usually happens is that the things at the end of the list get pushed back, and often, are left undone. This way of doing things drains a lot of energy, because we carry the dread of the things we avoid with us, and it weakens our will.

  To break through this bad habit, and increase your will,

choose first doing something you have been avoiding. When you have accomplished it, reward yourself. Let yourself know you did well. The next thing will be easier to do, until eventually, avoidance will stop being an issue, and you will not be piling up a list of unaccomplished tasks!

We tend to be inconsistent in the application of our will. For example, we may be very disciplined in our diet at home, yet we lose that discipline in the company of friends. That inconsistency undermines our will. It creates 'blind spots' where we fail to exercise our will out of habit or avoidance. Here is another checklist to help you discover where these areas may be for you and where you can recover your will:

Will Recovery Checklist – Areas in your life

How do you let go of your will within relationship? Part 1

- Do you make others responsible for your feelings or emotions?
- Do you have a tendency to blame others for your feelings?
- When things are not going the way you would like, do you keep relying on excuses and explanations to convince others, and yourself, that you had nothing to do with it, and that you are not to blame?

If the answer to any of these questions is yes, then make an effort to do the following:

Take complete responsibility for the way you feel. Take responsibility for admitting what has happened and for moving forward. Make sure that your conversations do not make the other person responsible for how you feel, and that you do not give your will away. Often, when we are reactive and give our will away, our very language holds that structure by making the other person the action or subject, and ourselves, the reaction (see examples below).

In the end, most people you interact with do not appreciate being the cause of your suffering, not matter how much you may wish to convince them. As a result, they are not likely to listen to what you have to say, and are more likely to put up a fight. If you want them to listen, begin speaking from your heart and owning your own will. Therefore, avoid saying things like:

"When you do this to me, I . . ."
"Because you do this to me, I . . ."
"You always do this to me."
"You never do this for me, that's why I . . ."

Express how you feel without blame. Talk about you, your dreams and what is in your heart, without judgments. Create actions and intentions that hold your will and do not give it away. Often, if you offer a win/win option, you are likely to get a win/win response. You might try saying:

"I feel this way. Let's do something about it!"
"This hurt. Is there a way we can resolve this?"

How do you let go of your will within relationship? Part 2

- Are you waiting for the other to make the first move?
- Are you waiting for them to fulfill an understanding or promise before you can act?
- Are you in a holding pattern with your will?

If the answer is yes to any of these questions, then make an effort to do the following:

Take an action that either breaks the ice or moves towards what you feel is appropriate. If necessary, create a new contract or understanding that doesn't place you in a holding pattern now, and apply this the next time.

Ask for what you want in a clear and non-judgmental way. Discuss what both of you want or are willing to do. Determine what it is that is holding you or your partner back. Ask. Find out. It may be that, both of you are waiting for the same thing, or there is a simple misunderstanding that can be cleared up.

How do you let go of your will at work? Part 1

- Do you delay asking for what you need?

If the answer is yes, then make an effort to do the following:

Take the time to consider your request and determine if it is appropriate and well presented. More often than not, the squeaky wheel gets the attention. If your request is legitimate then acknowledge that your own sense of limitations may be stopping you from asking. Often managers will ask you 'to tow the line' in principle, but are open to realistic requests. If you do not ask, not only are you unlikely to get what you need, you are also setting yourself up to be overlooked in the future. Ultimately, your productivity and self worth may suffer. Ask for what you need. Present your case clearly and in terms of how it will improve your contribution at work.

How do you let go of your will at work? Part 2

- Do you stay in a job that is not good for you?
- Have you stopped being open to good or better opportunities as they arise?

If the answer is yes to either question, then make an effort to do the following:

Take the time to consider what your prospects are for better jobs or positions. If you need training or preparation to attain the required skill sets, diplomas or certifications, then, what is stopping you from doing this preparation right now?

People often get caught in feeling that they are part of a big family at work, thus stop moving forward or upgrading themselves. Then, when there are layoffs or difficult times, the illusion that their situation is secure evaporates overnight. It is an illusion that your job will always protect you. You have to protect yourself and seek your own best interests. Don't become one of the people that give their will away to their job. Take back your will and stay youthful in terms of your prospects.

How do you let go of your will with friends?

- Do you stay in friendships that are not good for you?
- Do you hang out with individuals or groups that actually drain your time, energy and money without giving you back

a sense of excitement, of feeling alive or of sharing good times?

If the answer to either is yes, then make an effort to do the following simple exercise:

Take a piece of paper and make four vertical columns. In the first column, write a list of all the friends and acquaintances that you hang out with, leaving some space between their names. In the second column, next to each name, write down the positive effects of being around them. In the third column, write down the negative effects. Be honest with yourself. You are not judging them. You are simply jotting down the effects **on you** of being around them. When you are finished, go back to all of the names and give each a 'friendship' number, ranging from a perfect positive 10 to a neural 5 and an 'avoid at all cost', 0.

Now, for each name in the fourth column, write down why you spend time with this person. What are your needs that get met? Do you feel obligated? Why? What would happen if you stopped spending time with this person? What is happening to your will as you spend time with this person? Do you find yourself avoiding what you need to do and doing what is not good for you, on a regular basis, with this person? Be honest with yourself. It is your choice to spend time with people that drain your time and energy. Choose.

How do you let go of your will with food and company?

- Do you ignore your diet when you are with company?
- Do you normally intend to eat the food that is good for you, but tend to succumb to old patterns when you are with company, or especially with certain people?

If the answer to either is yes, then make an effort to do the following:

Make a list of what you can eat and the places that have the kind of food that is on your diet. Try to socialize in the places that support your diet preferences. If that doesn't work out, then make an effort to bring your own food with you. See if your friends will accommodate you. This is one way you can find out if they are really your friends. Decide what is important to you ahead of time and stick to your decision.

How do you let go of will with yourself?

- Do you succumb to the negative stories and responses that you play in your head? Are you a victim of the negative beliefs you hold of yourself?
- When you don't succeed with a task, do you put yourself down? Are you your worst critic?

If the answer is yes to any of these questions, then make an effort to do the following:

Make realistic goals for yourself. A good way to fail, and to feel that your will and ability to succeed amounts to nothing, is to take every opportunity to put yourself down. Then you can tell yourself: *"I know I failed because I am not good enough."*

Either you set your goals too high, or you like to fail and then blame yourself. Which is it? Set goals that you can achieve. It is your choice if you experience little success or even constant failure because you have set an unrealistic path to your goals. Do you need to break the process into smaller, more practical steps? Make realistic assessments of what you can do, and start there.

Every time you have a success, no matter how small, make every effort to let yourself know that you have succeeded, that you have done well. Know that the negative stories are just a bad habit. You can strengthen your will tremendously if you replace your negative stories with positive acknowledgements.

A post note

Often, regarding will, the difficulty is in taking the first step. Know that as soon as you take that first step, you will already be different. You are already on the journey of recovering your will and your personal power. Each action will change your perspective of how you see yourself and others. It is a process of positive change. Over time, the sense of obstacles will be replaced by a list of successes. It will be replaced by regained trust in yourself and in your ability to choose what is right for you.

Exercising your will is like exercising your muscles. After a while you become stronger and begin to enjoy greater challenges. Each time you choose to act for your own greater good, reward yourself. Acknowledge what you have done.

Chapter Summary

Our will is that part of us that keeps our integrity and ability to act. We give away our will when we become separated from our feelings and our heart making others responsible for our growth, joy and integrity. We regain our will when we exercise it and use it towards our own integrity, feelings and worth. As we apply our will, our trust in ourselves grows and our will strengthens.

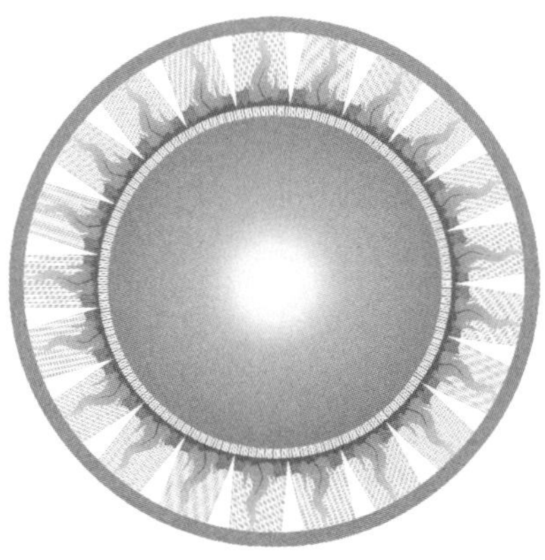

The Ego

One of the most misunderstood concepts that have resulted in the meeting between the west and the east, has been the idea of the ego. The ego has developed a very negative connotation, in some ways, as the embodiment of evil. We hear things such as: "*The ego must be destroyed*" or "*The ego must be made subservient to the will,*" or, in order to reach the experience of the divine, "*The ego must be sacrificed.*" These ideas have no real foundation, yet they have taken root in our beliefs about our selves. How has this happened?

Part of the explanation lies in the fact that in the West, the means and techniques for healing the injuries to the soul and the personality, are quite new developments. There is no long established popular tradition of being with a spiritual teacher that can remove the thorns that have accumulated in the student. Many of the injuries to the personality that we find in the West are much more rare in the East, and so the teachings that Westerners receive from the East tend not to address this area.

In fact, for many of the peoples of the world, the lower three chakras, (subtle energy centers dealing with survival, sex and power or ego) are often not focused on, as it is assumed that the person is fine and that both the culture and the family experience does not reject healthy functioning here. On the other hand, many Westerners, in trying to reach spiritual heights, get caught by unprocessed or un-integrated early childhood issues. It is like someone trying to do a high jump in wet blue jeans. It can be a sorry sight.

The truth is that we need our egos.

We cannot function in society or in the world without egos. It is our own ego that maintains our integrity in actions and goals. We could not feed ourselves or sustain a livelihood without ego. The only way that it is possible for you to stay alive without an ego, is for there to be a support system to take care of you, day and night. In some cultures, there is this support system. There are traditions of feeding mendicant monks and ecstatic beings that depend on the love of others for the necessities of life. In our culture, it is our egos that keep us from walking in front of a speeding car, or that can sustain a job to feed ourselves. There is nothing wrong with having an ego. In fact, it is very good to have an ego.

The issue is not even about whether you have a good ego or a bad ego. The issue is whether your ego works for you or against you, whether you have a useful, healthy and strong ego, or whether your ego wastes your time, energy and opportunities. A healthy ego helps you in the process of growing and maturing and making the choices necessary for a fulfilling and great life. An unhealthy or weak ego undermines such efforts and puts you down. In a way, an ego is an image of yourself that you hold and that sustains you through each new moment. A healthy ego is a great thing, a great accomplishment. It creates a positive influence, a positive integration. Most great beings did not become great without great egos.

Imagine two people. One believes himself to be not different than the sun, feeling that he shines with his own radiance, that he is the light, and he offers that radiance, enthusiasm and heartfulness to everyone around him. The other believes himself to be very pious. He tells everyone he meets how unworthy he is. Where do you see these two in ten years? They both have big egos. One has an ego that sustains not only itself, but also the people around him. The other has an ego that needs others to sustain it. A healthy ego can sustain great things. An unhealthy ego can be a thief, not only to its possessor, but to the people in its presence that keep being called upon to support it.

Selfishness and self-centeredness

Why then do we put the ego down? We do so for the same reasons that we put ourselves and others down. It is very convenient to tell a child that they are doing something wrong when they are taking care of themselves but not doing what the parents want. It can be an everyday occurrence, where a child standing up for her own experience or truth, challenges what the parent believes. The child is asked to stand down, to sacrifice their own truth, in order to please the parent. Otherwise, the child is being selfish! This is how an unhealthy ego is created. The child has learned to take care of the parent's ego, at the price of her own. And when this person has their own children, they will often treat them the same way they were treated, repeating the cycle.

We propagate the very bad egos we claim to be preventing. We hold back the natural development of healthy egos for the convenience of parents and culture. However, the culture and the parents usually pay a great price for supporting someone who does not support themselves.

True selfishness occurs when people act from an unhealthy and limited ego, one that is less connected to the heart and feeds off of others to sustain it. Such selfishness occurs, because the ego cares for nothing but itself, to feed itself. This is often noticed when people seek the center of attention at the price of others, or when there is a lack of sharing or compassion — all symptoms of a lack of heart.

However, selfishness can hide in the other extreme — being too nice to others. It is still selfishness, because others are being asked to sustain a need to be nice, others are still paying a price.

It is the price of someone not willing to take responsibility and not willing to be in their own heart, in their own truth and courage, and instead constantly needing others for acceptance, courage and will.

Selfishness must never be confused with self-centeredness, with being centered in one's self, with being centered and connected to one's heart. People who are centered in their self, in their core and in their heart, not only take care of themselves, but they are a beacon to inspire others.

The purpose of an ego

The ego connects each moment of our awareness with the preceding moment. In a way, it started as a kind of survival routine. You learned what was safe, what needed to be avoided, what worked for you and what did not. In a way, the ego became a kind of virtual reality that mimicked the world around you so that you could anticipate situations, learn and respond more effectively. After a while, the ego took on more and more tasks, and began to separate you from experiencing the world as it is, and instead, led you towards experiencing what you have come to believe.

Let me tell you the good news and the bad news about your ego. The good news is that you are not your ego. You are much, much greater than the ego can even imagine. That's the good news. The bad news is that your ego thinks it is all there is. It thinks it's you! The ego is like an assistant that over time has taken on the roles of receptionist, security, general manager, and now it wants to be the boss! You have to take the responsibility to put it back in its place. No one else will do it for you. The catch is that your ego is quite happy to do this for you, if you let it.

However, your ego will not connect you to your heart, it is not the source of joy, and it will not take you there. People often make the mistake of trying to get past the ego, using the ego. It doesn't work that way, unless you want your assistant to be your boss.

What causes our ego to work against us?

Our ego becomes our closest enemy, when it begins to hold thoughts, ideas, beliefs and resonances about ourselves that tend to bring us down, that undermine who we are. Our ego becomes this way because it is influenced by what people say to us; their beliefs, their attitudes and judgments about us.

Let's take the same analogy of the company, with our ego as the receptionist and the office staff. Can you imagine how a company can get into trouble if most of their staff held negative beliefs and attitudes about their employer? Over time, it will significantly undermine the ability of the company to function successfully. Other companies may even take advantage of the lack of loyalty.

When we accept the definitions others place on us, and we adapt to the beliefs of others, our ego begins to act like an instrument that undermines us and holds us back. In a sense, it is as if our ego has sold us out and became our enemy.

How can our ego become our friend?

Our ego connects our past, present and future. In some ways, it is the architect and chief administrator of these divisions of how we view ourselves and the world. The ego is concerned with giving us continuity and protecting us from making mistakes. It holds on to beliefs about ourselves, even when they are negative. Our ego tends to bring us back to how we were yesterday and the day before. It holds our continuity for us. When we try to change, it is our ego that acts to bring us back. It is difficult to change who we are if we use this aspect of ourselves to initiate or to maintain that change. So, what can we do to change all of this? How can we get the ego to work for us?

The ego learns through repetition. It believes very easily, the same way that a small child believes. This should not come as a surprise, because the ego formed when we were little. The ego protects what it believes, otherwise, we would not hold on to what we learn, or we would not learn from our mistakes.

The trick is to work with the ego, in the way it likes to work; with continuity, maintaining consistency, keeping us within the range of safety and comfort. If we push the ego, it pushes back to realign. If we pull the ego along, it will go along for the ride.

Our ego likes to ingest information that it can hold; images, phrases, beliefs and ideas. Therefore, the easiest way to work with the ego is to feed it ideas and beliefs that you want it to hold and protect.

Most people know that they are influenced by their interactions with others, by what others say and do, and by their reactions to these things. Most people ignore, or do not realize that our own ego is just as influenced by what we say and do. Therefore, say and do the things that create positive beliefs and images to feed your ego.

This is much simpler and easier to do than it may seem; all that is needed is to catch yourself when you are down on yourself, when you are negative, when you put yourself down. Each time you catch your ego saying something negative about you, give your ego something positive to say instead.

Let's go back to our analogy of the company. The receptionist tells the boss that things are bad – this is the gossip they picked up a year ago, but nothing has been heard to change that impression, and so the receptionist keeps saying it. Some bosses would just shrug and repeat what they heard. *"Yea, I've heard it before, yep."* Some bosses are just yes-men to their staff, and to the staff opinions. This is a company run by the mail room, by gossip. This is a company without a leader.

It doesn't have to be that way! In fact, the staff is waiting for input and leadership from the boss. It is because this input was missing, that things drifted the way they did.

If the boss were to say, *"Hey, listen, that's what our competitor once said. It's invalid. We're doing fine, pass it on."* The next time, the receptionist is likely to pass on the latest gossip: *"Guess what I just heard? We're doing fine, did you know?"*

It is that simple. Catch yourself, each time you hear a negative impression, replace it with a positive one. It works! Be the boss. It's what a good boss would do. Do it, and keep doing it.

The image that you hold of yourself will improve. When a whole company becomes more positive about itself, it will be much more willing to take the appropriate actions to expand and succeed. Its positive attitude about itself will be contagious. The receptionists of other companies will start to spread the rumor of how great this company is. It would be time to buy stock in this company!

A word about truth

Some of you may take the position that if you are saying something positive about yourself, when you believe that the negative statement holds more truth for you, then you are not speaking your truth. This is not about the truth as a static belief, or even about the validity of what you hold yourself to be. It is about maintaining the belief and trust in yourself that keeps the doors to life open.

People that are positive about themselves tend to attract and take advantage of positive experiences and opportunities. People that are negative about themselves, tend to push away joy and success. Which is the truth, being positive or being negative?

Ultimately the truth flows like a river. It is alive. When it stops flowing, when it ceases to be alive, it no longer holds benefit; it becomes dry and begins to stand in the way of experiences and choices that bring life.

Allowing yourself to be positive welcomes you to your potential and welcomes life and experience. You are much more open to what is offered. Truth is what brings you closer to your heart and to your positive potential. Holding negative beliefs about yourself is not the truth. It is a falsehood that does not ring true to your real nature. Hold the truth that sets you free.

In order to help you move closer to being the boss of your ego, here is a short checklist.

Be the Boss checklist

1. Do you put yourself down because you feel you could have

done better?

- If you do, chances are that even if you did it perfectly, you would find a way to put yourself down. Instead, acknowledge what you did. What would you say if someone else did it? A good boss lets their people know that mistakes are tolerated as part of learning to do things better.
- Acknowledge several good things that you did. If there is room for improvement, consider it, write it down, and then acknowledge yourself for learning to improve and spend the energy and time preparing for the next task.

2. Do you get up in the morning with a sense of doom and gloom?
   - Do you expect things to go wrong? Some people are afraid of expecting good things because they feel that, if they set up positive expectations, it will somehow jinx things or set them up for failure. Unfortunately, expecting negative things usually invites them.
   - To break through this, do what very successful people do. They wake up rejoicing each new day for the treasures and victories it will bring. The ancient Romans had an expression 'Seize the day.' Imagine yourself victorious. Imagine that something good will happen. Imagine that a gift will come your way and see if you can discover it. When you reach out for a good day, often that is what you will get in return. You are the boss. Seize the day.

3. Start dining on good thoughts.
   - Many people that overeat, or eat late, are trying to fill a void, a need. Often this void is created with negative thoughts, and people try to fill this void with comforting food. You can fill that void with positive thoughts just as easily, and with great savings to your wallet and figure! Recall some of the great and heartfelt things that have happened to you.
   - Make a list of the positive thoughts you need to dine on, and enjoy.

4. Notice and appreciate your lessons.
   - Often, when we have difficulty with someone else or with a situation, it is actually telling us something about ourselves. It is letting us know where we need to do more work on ourselves. Many people tend to cast blame or responsibility when they are not getting what they want. Successful people tend to see such situations as a challenge to improve themselves.
   - To grow and meet our challenges usually requires that we give something away in order to make room for growth. If things are not working out, find out what is holding you back. Find out what it is in you, rather than in someone else, that needs to be looked at. Find out what you can let go of in order to move forward and what needs to shift in a positive direction to meet the challenge that is offered. In this way, the challenge becomes a gift from the universe to help you be greater. It is often said that we learn from our mistakes. This is partly because we notice what doesn't work, and we do something about it.

> *Whether you think you can or think you can't,*
> *you're right.*
>
> Henry Ford

> *We either make ourselves miserable,*
> *or we make ourselves strong.*
> *The amount of work is the same.*
>
> Carlos Castaneda

Chapter Summary

In this chapter we looked at the ego as a necessary instrument of being in the world. The chapter focused on making the ego your friend and how to take over responsibility for your ego so that it can work for you. It is important to catch your ego when it holds negative concepts and beliefs about you and to replace these with positive acknowledgements that are of benefit. It is also important to get into the habit of acknowledging your success, and to train your ego to be a support for you.

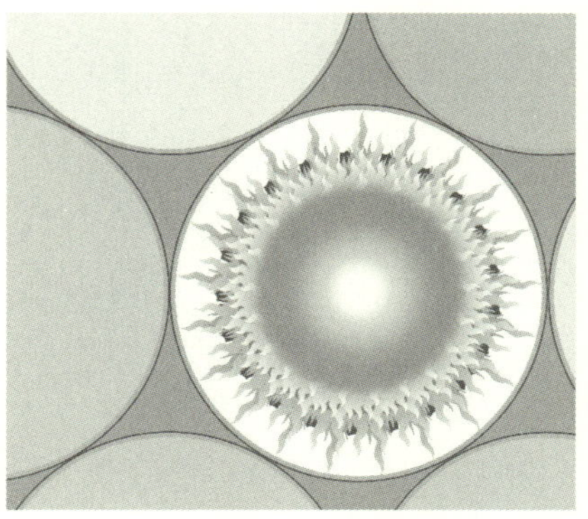

Direction
Knowing what is in your heart

Knowing what you want

If you don't know what you want, then chances are that you are doing what someone else wants.

If it is difficult for you to uncover what you want, then you have removed yourself from your true feelings, or you have covered these feelings up. The consequence of not knowing what you want is that you become adrift and lose your direction, and this means that you are not moving towards your goals, dreams and needs.

Some people have great difficulty expressing their needs, wants and desires. They sometimes go for years in a relationship waiting for the other to change so that what they want from their partner will magically appear or become possible.

Life has an interesting way of manifesting our dreams and prayers. When we hide from what we want, what we want tends to be hidden from us. If we seek it out even through the tiniest steps, we tend to move towards our desires, or what we want moves closer to us. It depends on the direction we take, and whether that direction is aligned with our heart. When we know what is in our heart, then we know what we want, and we can truly welcome our dreams and what life reveals for us. This chapter looks at the means to do just that.

Are you hiding what you want?

Are you hiding what is in your heart? Do you sometimes know what you want, but are afraid to ask? What stops you?

More often than not, what stops most people is the disconnection between their thinking and their feelings, between their head and their heart. The fear comes from being disconnected from the courage of living their joy and their truth.

We may know what we want with our head and our desires, but it is our separation from our feelings and heart that stops us. We come up against our fears and negative beliefs about ourselves, expressions of that very separation. We are stopped by our fears of rejection, worthlessness or our beliefs that what we want, won't happen.

As a result, when we ask from separation, and conflict between what we think and feel, we have already predetermined our fate. We are already placing the wrong foot forward. When we come from a place of expecting rejection, then often that is what we get.

Imagine a sales person coming to you and saying *"I have this product I am supposed to sell to you, but it doesn't really matter and its okay if you say no."* Imagine another sales person who approaches you and says, *"By the way, this is a great product, I personally endorse it, and I think you will really appreciate that I mentioned it to you."* Who is likely to get your business?

The hidden messages in not knowing what you want

Have you ever had a conversation with people who need something from you, but won't tell you what it is? You know they want something from you. It would be helpful if they simply said something, yet when you ask them, the reply is that they do not know!

It can be frustrating to experience someone asking for something on the one hand, and denying or hiding what they want. Children do this. You ask them what they want, and they sometimes say *"I don't know."*

It is frustrating to hear this, because it is a contradictory message. The outer message is *"I want something and it is important to me, but I can't tell you what it is."* The hidden message is, *"What I want is not important and I am not important."*

Having to hear such a contradictory message can place their friends in a predicament. People don't really want to accept such a stance. They do not want to be responsible for the others lack of importance, nor do they want to accept their hidden message. Even if they were to guess what this person really wants, the hidden message is a warning that this person is not in the right place to receive what may be offered, and people do not want to waste the goodness of their hearts.

When you are asked for money by someone at a street corner and you see this person smoking cigarettes, there may be greater reluctance to give away money if perceived it will be wasted. There is a reluctance to give something to someone who will not accept it properly. There is also a reluctance to give if the message is contradictory.

The hidden message, given to the universe, of not knowing what you want, is that you are not open or willing to receive what comes your way.

Trying to get what you want

People often hope and pray for what they want and may feel that because they do not manifest what they seek, the universe is trying to tell them something. That premise is correct. The universe is trying to tell them something, but more often than not, they are not hearing the right message. Instead, they are hearing their internal dialogue with disappointment.

Have you ever stopped and considered how people actually phrase their hopes and prayers?

Pay attention to what you ask

Phrasing is very important. I once witnessed an interesting exchange between a teacher and a student:

The student approached the teacher, and said: *"I am having great difficulty understanding the principle you talked about."*

The teacher replied: *"I really can't help you until you let go of your 'difficulty' in understanding. I can't help you until you get rid of your negative attitude. If you approached me, and said, please help me understand, or can you give me more clarity, I would be very glad to do so. However, you come to me with your inability to understand. Until you drop that, what can I do?"*

In real life, we often want something but are unwilling to let go of the very thing that keeps that possibility away. We often are not aware of how we stop ourselves from receiving what we want.

When people pray or express their hopes, it is usually worded in the same manner as that student. People say: *"I hope to be successful. Someday, I want to be rich and famous. If only people would like me."* These are the kinds of things that people say, and then they are surprised why they did not get what they asked for. Of course, the irony is that they did! Most people when they ask or pray, express a hidden message that contradicts what they purport to seek.

The hidden message

Let's look at the above examples a little more closely, to reveal their hidden message.

If someone says *"I hope to be successful,"* they are saying, in effect, *"I do not see myself successful, I only put out the possibility in the future, but I am really holding on to my non-success in this moment that I ask."* And of course, the universe replies back, *"Okay, I hear you – you are choosing to hold on to non-success and you have hopes – Granted!"*

If someone says: *"Someday, I want to be rich and famous,"* they are saying in effect: *"I do not relate to being rich and famous in the moment in which I ask for it. I only have a vague sense of a future where I will want this."* And of course, the universe replies back: *"Okay, I hear you – you are choosing to hold on to not being rich and famous in the present and you also want to hold on to the wanting to be rich and famous in the future– Granted!"*

If someone says: *"If only people would like me,"* they are saying in effect, *"I am not willing to let go of being unlikable in the moment that I am asking, and I am only expressing a regret."* And of course, the universe replies back: *"Okay, I hear you – you are choosing to hold on to not being liked in the present and you have regrets that you would like to extend into the future – Granted!"*

Does any of this sound familiar to you? How would you reword those phrases so that they would have effect? Just as an exercise, consider the following restatements: *"I am successful, I am rich and famous, I am likeable and I invite others to experience this in me."*

In the same way that we may show hidden messages in our hopes and prayers, we tend to do so in almost all interactions with others, with ourselves and with the world. It is little wonder that the results come the way they do! We say things like: *"I want money, or I need money, or there isn't enough money,"* more often than *"I welcome money"* or even *"I love money."*

The hidden messages we give other people

In our relationships with the people around us, there is opportunity for hidden messages beyond just words. There is body language, eye contact and the tone of our voice. These can carry our double messages to confuse another person in terms of what we actually want. The point is that many of us tend to put up obstacles in the process of asking. And if we don't catch ourselves, we tend to communicate these obstacles with more clarity then we communicate what we want.

Why would we do this? Often it is because we want two things that we are disguising as one. On the one hand, we are asking for something that we purport to want. On the other hand, we are seeking acceptance for a part of ourselves that has difficulty asking, and that we ourselves have difficulty accepting. That part of ourselves may be waiting to be healed, acknowledged and even appreciated. That part of us may exist due to emotions and hurts from a past experience that we have not yet healed or dealt with. In a previous chapter, we have seen how emotions hold disconnections from our core and from our heart, they interfere when we ask for what we want. When you notice that interference, take the opportunity to heal that disconnection. It is revealing itself to you for a reason.

Here is a list of things you can do to help you not get what you want. Some of these may be familiar to you. See if you can discover the disconnection or hidden message that is revealing itself.

Ways to avoid getting what you want.

- Don't ask for what you want.
- Be indirect.
- Make the other person responsible for guessing what you want.
- Keep telling them that it doesn't matter.
- Don't be connected to your heart and feelings.
- Expect to be disappointed.
- Ask for what you want from a contracted, unlovable or rejected place.
- Make the other person responsible for accepting you as small or unworthy.
- Make it difficult for other people to give you things.
- Don't accept gifts with warmth and thankfulness.
- Tell them they shouldn't have given you what they have.
- Tell them that you are not worthy of it.

Getting what you want

How do we turn things around? How do we ask in such a way that we increase our chances of success? The answer is simple. We have to believe in ourselves. When we believe in ourselves, our message and our request is coherent, positive and more easily accepted by others.

I know people who are very positive about themselves and about life. Often, when they are buying something, they ask for a better price. They do so warmly, with no emotional agenda. They do not put themselves or others down. They feel very comfortable asking. Their stance is that of course this is a reasonable thing to do. Most of the time, they get a better price! They get what they want, and the sales people actually feel good in granting it!

Why does this happen? Partly, it is because these people are sharing their joy and people respond positively to joy. Partly, it is because, this honest, playful request is such a relief compared to all of the other demands that customers have placed, that the sales person can't resist a chance to play.

This is the secret to getting what we want. The secret lies in being ourselves, being in our hearts, in our feelings, and acting from that place. For many people, someone coming playfully from the heart is as difficult to resist as a newborn infant. From this place, our direction in life tends to unfold naturally and with the support of those around us.

Let the world know you as you are,
not as you think you should be.

Fannie Brice

Chapter summary

In this chapter we looked at the relationship of knowing, and choosing our direction in life based on our connection with our heart. When we ignore our feelings and who we are, we tend to be adrift, and thus are open to being caught up in the needs of others. We guarantee that we will not get what we need or want, when we deny to ourselves and to others, our desires and needs, when we avoid asking, or when we ask in a way that places the responsibility or blame on others. Success comes from asking and engaging from our feelings and from the stance of our heart.

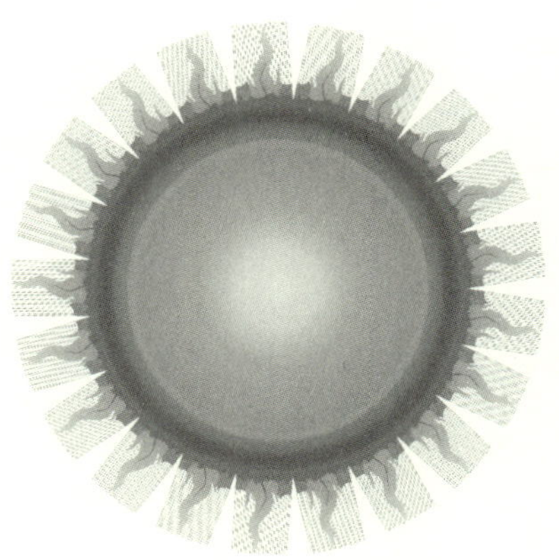

Sin

Separation from your Inner Nature

This chapter takes another look at the process of regaining your power from the perspective of your integrity.

The nature of sin

In Western cultures, sin is the act of doing something that is wrong, that does harm, or is of negative merit. It is also the accumulation of bad merit. You are asked to be good, to do the right thing and follow your conscience. Sin happens when you deviate from what is good in your community or society.

In Eastern cultures, sin can be roughly translated as actions that take you out of appropriateness, or away from the right path. The right path or way is called Dharma, Righteousness, the Tao, or being in Grace. Here, sin happens when you deviate from what is good for you.

Have you ever wondered what it is about sin that makes it wrong? Sin holds our disconnection to our heart or our core. Sin is that which causes us to forget and ignore our inner connection, and instead, binds us outwardly to an attachment. Sin separates us from our own hearts. We hold on to this separation, to the memories and experiences that created it, and to the sense of unworthiness and shame resulting from it. The damage of sin is that it holds that separation, keeping us from being vital, truly present and open to the unfolding of our life.

What keeps us in sin?

Most people are forced by circumstance to choose between their inner and outer sense of integrity. They are asked to choose between what they feel is right and what others expect of them. It is not an easy choice. It is rarely a win/win situation, because for most people, the choice is about fear. It is about what they fear the most.

Most people fear being judged and losing the validation, acceptance and support of the people in their lives, more than they fear losing their own integrity. That this choice is based on fear, already means, that their connection to their inner integrity, to their heart and true feelings, has already been compromised. The price of continuing to enjoy this type of outer acceptance and relationship is, to deny the inner connection and inner relationship.

This is partly what keeps us in sin. We do what is pragmatic, politically expedient, practical, appeasing and what is demanded of us. We protect our outer integrity; the way others perceive, acknowledge and judge us. We want to be 'good' on the outside and try to keep our 'word' with others. However, our inner relationships, our feelings, our integrity and our core are sacrificed, and in keeping this outer 'peace' we often break our 'word' with ourselves. That sacrifice separates us from our sense of being good on the inside, as it can put a wedge between who we identify ourselves to be and our joy. That experience of separation can act as a wound needing to be healed and we hold on to the experiences that created this wound, in the form of emotions, guilt and shame. All this keeps us in sin.

How do emotions keep us in sin?

We blame others for the wounds that we carry. As long as we blame them, we tie up our own will and our own ability to free our selves from our wounds by taking the right actions that might heal us. Instead, we get caught in churning over our past issues like an inner morality play — "*They did this*," or "*I was a victim*," or "*How could they do this to me?*" We run these morality plays in our minds. They support our hope that we are right and they are wrong, that they are responsible and we are not! It supports our unwillingness to heal ourselves, and thus, we maintain our separation from our core. We keep ourselves in sin.

How does guilt and shame keep us in sin?

Guilt is the awareness of using our will inappropriately. We know that we did something that separated ourselves from our core and from our heart. We know we gave our will away. We know we did wrong; we felt it while we did it. We know that we did something that disconnected us from our integrity and truth, and this guilt holds our loss of will.

Where does the will go? It goes in the direction of blame. However, instead of blaming others, we blame ourselves for what we have done. We hold a sense of responsibility for having allowed a disconnection from our spirit, our soul and our heart. Unfortunately, that blame keeps us down. It continually maintains our separation from our core.

Shame is our experience of contraction that resulted in our separation from our core and integrity. It is closely allied with fear. Our shame maintains our own hiding from our core and our hearts. It immobilizes us in the same way that fear does, as our experience of separation.

What we need to realize is that we are holding on to the effects of being disconnected from our core. We are judging ourselves by our disconnection, not by our hearts. It is our shock of disconnection that we hold through guilt and shame. As long as we hold that shock, we maintain separation from who we really are.

How does misguided responsibility keep us in sin?

We may hold our guilt and shame because we accept responsibility for it; we may even hold the misguided notion that it is appropriate to suffer, because we have committed a 'sin.' We may believe that suffering is the punishment for our actions and choices. This is a blatant wrong sense of responsibility, because here we are choosing responsibility for the separation from our hearts, rather than for reconnecting to our hearts! It is our responsibility to heal our connection to our hearts: holding on to the wounds and suffering is irresponsible. When we do this, we suffer and wonder why! The universe is trying to let us know!

How does blaming others keep us in sin?

Something happened to disconnect us from our core, from our heart. Perhaps it is the result of a challenging event, or of something someone did to us. Even though we got hurt, our separation from our core and our heart was ultimately our choice. No one else can actually do this. We are the only ones that can choose to hide from our inner light and joy. We are the only ones that can hide from our hearts. We are ultimately responsible for that choice. We are the ones that have to live through its consequences.

When we do not take responsibility for losing our heart connection, we make others responsible. We hold others responsible for our suffering and we blame them instead of reasserting our own responsibility and will. We may hold the sense that 'they did this to us,' or that we hurt because of what 'they did.'

As long as we continue to blame others or make them responsible for our hurts and actions, we give them power over us and over our hearts. In this way, we delay taking back our own power and will to heal ourselves, and in that delay, we continue to hold our dis-integrity, our sin.

How do we free ourselves?

The first task we need to give ourselves in order to let go of our 'sin,' is to take responsibility for our actions. Various spiritual and healing traditions achieve this through confession, truthfulness, inner dialogue, self-acceptance and forgiveness.

The price of admission

Our journey to freedom starts by admitting to ourselves what we have done what caused us not to be in our hearts. Only an open admission begins the process of welcoming a part of ourselves home. Most people know this open admission as 'confession.'

The act of 'confession' is not just a purging of our inner responsibility to somebody else, or to a higher power; it is not about somebody else carrying our weight or our responsibility. In fact, this is where some people get stuck! Getting unstuck requires that we own responsibility for our actions and our selves. It requires realizing and acting upon the fact that we must live our own lives, as no one else can live it for us. For that reason alone, we are ultimately responsible, in that what happens in our lives, happens to us!

The true act of 'confession' is very much a process of re-alignment, of standing firmly on the foundation of the truth of our actions and choices. It is saying, *"Here is where I lost my way with my own integrity; here is where I chose the wrong path, action, or intention."* It is an acknowledgement of what is, and more importantly, a reconnection to our integrity.

This act of confession is affirms our choice and our responsibility. Through this action, we are then freed to make the right choice of intention and action from our heart. From the place of our humility, from the place of our own truth, we reach out to the part of us which earlier disconnected by performing a regretted action, and through forgiveness, we re-welcome that part.

Forgiving ourselves

Forgiveness is about reconnecting to your heart, after separation. Forgiveness is the authentic act that resolves the past, allowing you to return to and live in the present moment.

Forgiveness is the healing process of reconnection, yet most people expect forgiveness to occur only on the outside; when we forgive others, or they forgive us. What we seem to truly forget is that forgiveness is not about making someone else responsible for actions that have resulted in disconnection from our integrity. Like confession, forgiveness is also a process to regain our own responsibility.

Where forgiveness gets stuck

Forgiveness is not about waiting for another to say they are sorry for what they did, before you can go on with your own life, or in order to be able to forgive them. First of all, it can be difficult for people to admit they may have been wrong, and, it is pointless to wait for years while holding emotional pain to be healed by someone else's recanting.

Even if they apologize, even if they admit that they were wrong, it may not be as healing as you may have hoped. Why? Because, for someone to truly repent in a way that can heal you, it requires that their authentic remorse reach to the depths of where you got hurt. True remorse and regret at this level, are rare.

Many people are caught in this waiting process. Most people, when they experience hurt from the actions of another, continually hold that person responsible for the pain they experience. We say things like "*He did this to me*!" or "*She hurt my feelings!*" By making someone else responsible, we are giving them power over us; we maintain a reactive stance, as if we had no choice or power over the situation. We anxiously wait for them to say they are sorry, to change, to feel remorse for what they did. We wait. We wait to feel better. We wait to heal.

The problem is that in waiting for someone else to change,

we continue to hold ourselves in a reactive posture, we continue to make someone else responsible and we continue to give them power over us until the moment they repent. We have accepted a holding pattern, we have accepted giving away our power and responsibility to another, and all this keeps us stuck in our wound, our hurt. It is in fact, a huge part of the wound.

Forgiveness is not about making someone else responsible

It may seem fairly easy to accept that we need to take responsibility for our feelings if someone says something mean to us. But, it may not be so easy to accept the stance of responsibility when it comes to more extreme situations.

You may ask, "*What happens when someone is abused, or beaten up? How is it possible that they can be responsible for that? They did nothing wrong! An assault on their integrity came from others — so how can that be their responsibility?*"

Please bear with me as I try to explain. Most of these extreme examples involve people pressing their power over others. Often, the turning point in this power struggle is the reaction from the victim. As soon as someone becomes reactive, emotional, pleading, or acquiescing, they are in a process of accepting their own lack of power and the other's power over them. Often, for perpetrators who themselves may not feel empathy or have disconnected from their heart entirely, it is the taking of power that is their true reward. The demonstration of a victim's powerlessness is what they seek, in order to experience their own power. For the victims, part of the injury is an inner sense of guilt and shame for having acquiesced or allowed the abuse to happen. Part of the injury is knowing they chosen powerlessness and fear.

In order to heal and regain lost power, one needs to accept responsibility for having chosen to give power away, regardless of the circumstances. You need to forgive yourself for having done so. By taking responsibility and reclaiming your power, and, by forgiving yourself for giving it away, you can re-welcome your power into your life and break away from the trap of being a victim. Otherwise, the perpetrator will continue to hold your disowned power over you and healing will continue to be delayed.

Abuse is truly an extreme situation. However, if you look carefully at your own wounds, you are likely to find a demonstration of power and powerlessness right there. For example, let's say your peers made fun of you. You accepted the situation because you did not feel powerful enough to challenge it — perhaps you were not willing to risk upping the ante. Perhaps the power held over you by members of your group, felt like rejection, so you acquiesced. You now harbor resentment, anger, pain, even fear. What is it that you are still holding? This: You gave your power away; You chose to go along with an outer action that contradicted your inner integrity; You did not stand up for your inner integrity; You did not choose your responsibility for yourself on the inside. You chose fear and you gave away your power. That is the foundation of your hurt, your wound. In order to heal, you need to retake responsibility. That is the way back to your power.

Forgiveness is overcoming the hurt of being forsaken

Next, we are going to take a bit of a leap, so please bear with me! The experience of being hurt occurs on two levels, or places. One place tends to be the center of focus, the action done by the other person. The other place is often ignored as it happens inside, where the real hurt takes place.

Let's say someone approaches you and says or does something very mean to you and your 'feelings' get hurt. How did that person manage to hurt you? How did you get hurt?

You get hurt when you make what someone says or does, more important than your own connection to your heart. In a sense, you forsake your own centeredness, integrity and your own connection to your heart in the process of reacting to what is said or done. Maybe what was said or done made you question your integrity, and it became too painful to experience it while staying connected to your heart.

You experience that separation from your heart as fear and

anger, and as the giving away of your will and responsibility. You choose not to be responsible for your separation from your heart. You choose to make the perpetrator responsible. In the process of reacting to what you feel is being 'done' to you, you give away your will and power.

In the example above, when the other person tried to use power over you, with outer words or actions, you got nailed for giving up your own power, on the inside. You alone are responsible for what you did, because ultimately you chose to abandon yourself and let go of the connection to your own heart! **That is the wound: to abandon your self and your own heart.** You may make another responsible and blame him, but you alone are holding that wound. That is the hurt. It is now up to you to overcome that hurt and re-connect to your own heart.

Forgiveness is taking back your responsibility and power. You need to face that wound if you are to heal. You are responsible for letting go of your inner connection, and are equally responsible for bringing it back. To heal yourself, you have to untie or cut the knot that binds you - your acceptance of having given away your responsibility and power.

Untying the knot that binds

So, how do you take back your responsibility and power? By taking the first steps: acknowledging what happened, noticing how it affected you and realizing who truly gave away your power. If you allow yourself to look closely, you will find that somewhere in the process you gave away your own power. You did this. You may have felt that you had no choice, and perhaps there were not many choices available. Nevertheless, you did it, and you felt less powerful, powerless, as a result.

Bear in mind that you did not actually give power away. Instead, you took a stance of powerlessness. You still have your power, yet because of your stance, because you may still be holding on to the demonstration of powerlessness, you continue to give it away. You may be giving away your power, or responsibility, by holding your sense of being hurt, being the victim, holding fear, by waiting for another to say they are sorry, or by waiting for them to receive punishment.

Taking back your power

You have to take your power back! It's your power. It never left you. It is temporarily being used against you through your own choice.

To take back your power, you must forgive yourself! "*For what*?" you might ask. You must forgive yourself for giving your power away in the first place. You cannot wait for others to heal you by waiting for them to say they are sorry. You must heal yourself by letting yourself know that you are sorry for choosing acquiescence to the outer force of circumstances and to the detriment of your relationship with your core. Taking back your power means no longer embracing the state of powerlessness.

How do you manifest your responsibility? By taking appropriate care of your feelings, instead of hiding them, denying them or acting as if someone else's feelings are more important than yours. It may mean that a demonstration of your own power, or an affirmation that you are no longer choosing powerlessness, is necessary in some way. In the earlier example of being ridiculed in a group, that responsibility may take the form of standing up for your self from your truth, your power and strength — even if it is to say something non-reactive, but proactive and direct like "*Only a weak person needs to make themselves feel strong by making fun of another — you are losing my respect — keep this up, and soon you will lose everyone else's.*"

Becoming aware of your feelings is an important step in the recovery of power, because it can connect you to your heart and freedom. I repeat, **Becoming aware of your feelings is important because it connects you to your heart and freedom.** When recovering from traumatic situations, you need to feel your anger in order to be able to say, "*No more!" I am not going to let these people win by staying in a state of contraction — I am going to fight back and get my power back*". In these cases, you need to re-feel your anger, because it holds within it, your will. It is when you avoid feeling and taking back your will, that the anger becomes emotion and sin. In exercising your will in ways that are no longer reactive, but self-validating, you move towards healing.

The effects of forgiveness

Taking responsibility for re-welcoming your power opens the door to forgiving yourself for giving it up in the first place, crossing the path that may have become shrouded with inner guilt and shame, and releases their hold on your energy, thoughts and joy. The reconnection to your own integrity, your own heart, removes the nature of sin, which is the separation in the first place.

Forgiveness of yourself is a re-welcoming of your true nature, your joy, your lightness and willingness to participate in the present moment fully and not be held back by past issues. Forgiveness is really about reconnection; a willingness to accept yourself again, even though you may have once pushed a part of yourself away.

This is the meaning of the root of the word 'for-giveness' – giving of one's self, instead of waiting for the other to give before we are open to receive.

On the surface, it means breaking the ice, or making the move that re-connects, instead of waiting and holding the disconnection. People often want to see a demonstration of this when they see discord. They want to see the shaking of hands to end a conflict. What really matters though is what happens on the inside.

On the inside, forgiveness translates to breaking the holding energy pattern of hurt, separation or shame — the inner ice. It means reaching back to our own heart. It means reaching out towards the part of us that got hurt, and welcoming home, not only that part, but also our power. When we welcome both parts of ourselves home, we heal; they become 'us' again, not something done to us. The hurt and pain begin to release, as their only real purpose was the demonstration of the separation we once felt.

Self-forgiveness re-welcomes and re-aligns us to our core and breaks the yoke of past hurts, freeing us to move forward, bringing us back to the stance where we can be open to what the universe has to offer. This is why, in the west, self-forgiveness precedes communion; and why in the east, it is part of the preparation that makes a seeker worthy to receive.

Making guilt and shame our friends

You may have a sense of guilt when you are performing actions that separate you from your outer commitments, responsibilities or agreements.

In our relationships with other people, we also avoid placing ourselves into an experience of shame. That shame is an experience of separation from the approval or acceptance of others, and can take the form of humiliation or public loss of stature or position. That shame can bind our sense of guilt, and often the two go hand in hand.

It is very important to realize that these kinds of guilt and shame are learned. They come from adapting to the needs and demands of people and the world around us. For many, the source may be a family history of guilt being used as a weapon or tactic of manipulation, to force you in a direction that someone else wants or needs, and away from the direction you would choose.

These experiences of guilt and shame do not take us to our hearts. Instead they often pull us away from our hearts and our own integrity.

There are experiences of guilt or shame that are not learned. We experience these on the inside, when we lose connection with our integrity or when we choose to go against our nature, our core, our spirit or our heart. In this way, we experience inner guilt when we say or do something that is false for ourselves and when we swim against the current of the flow of our joy.

We experience inner shame when we become separated from our core, when we perform actions that pull us out of our direct connection with our hearts.

Both inner guilt and inner shame let us know immediately

that we are making the wrong choices in our lives and for our hearts. In a sense, they are pain at the level of our spirit. We learn to avoid touching something hot, because of the immediate sensation of pain. In the same way, inner guilt and shame make us aware that we are doing something against our own integrity.

It is important that we pay attention and act appropriately when we experience our inner guilt and shame. Like true friends, they let us know when we are off track. They let us know where we need to heal and where we are giving away our power.

It is only when we are disconnected from our own hearts and core, and after we have ignored our inner guilt and shame, that we become open targets of outer guilt and shame.

Self-trust is the essence of heroism.

Ralph Waldo Emerson

Chapter Summary

In this chapter, we examined the nature of sin as separation from our integrity, heart and core, and how we hold this separation through misplaced guilt and shame. We examined the process of self-forgivess as a means to heal and to regain our power and joy. We looked at the wounds we hold as an opportunity to identify the issues and to reconnect to the heart. Finally, we examined inner guilt and shame as immediate feedback telling us when we lose integrity with our heart or core.

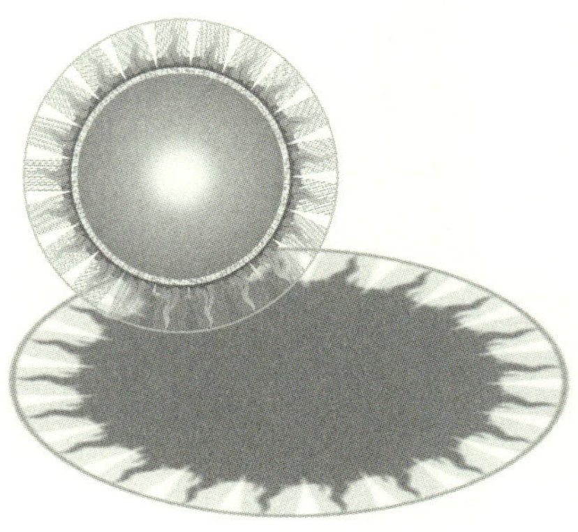

Responsibility

Who carries the responsibility for your life?

Life is a promise, fulfill it.

Mother Teresa

There are two kinds of responsibility. The first kind of responsibility is a given. We are born with it. It is our own responsibility for our life, for how we feel, for what we experience and what we do with our lives. No one can take this responsibility away from us. It is our life. We are the ones that ultimately experience it and reap the rewards and consequences of our actions.

The second kind of responsibility is learned. Someone taught us to do the chores, to take out the garbage, to go to school and later to work. These were not the choices we would have made had we not been forced to accept rules, regulations and commitments. Although we may seek to avoid or even rebel from this kind of responsibility, this is not where the greatest difficulties with responsibility lie.

The problem with responsibility occurs when we forget our primary responsibility to ourselves. It is no wonder that this happens, because we are rarely reminded to do so. The pull instead is to be responsible outside of ourselves, and ultimately, to do what others want us to do. For our family, employers, teachers and even our friends, there is little payoff when we start taking care of and honoring ourselves!

Honoring yourself

Honoring begins by honoring the present moment. Are you honoring yourself in how you live each moment? How do you conduct your life? Are you being responsible to yourself?

When we do not honor our selves we tend to accumulate debts. To regain our honoring of ourselves, it is necessary to regain control of debt and the way we accumulate debt. This is not just the debt of money owed, but the debt of obligation, expectation and commitment that was made when we did not honor ourselves. Otherwise, obligations that we have made and money that we owe, can steal from the opportunities that life offers us in the present moment, by pulling us into the past.

We alone are responsible for the fullness of the present moment, and in order for us not to lose our birthright of joy, we need to act in our own benefit, always. We need to free ourselves of the debts we have accumulated, both monetary and emotional. It is vital to start taking care of business today, not tomorrow. Successful people do not put off what they can do today. For this reason, a schedule or organizing method of some sort can be invaluable to deal with what needs to be done, and to protect your personal time. If you need help, get it. There are agencies and organizations that help people successfully free themselves of debt. Do what you need to do to become responsible for the present. It is important. Otherwise your present will belong to others.

Not minding your business

A western medicine man once told me this story:

One day a man was walking through the forest and he felt very good. He felt the need to share that feeling and to perform positive gestures for others. As he was passing a large rock, he noticed that a small tree seemed to be struggling around its edge, and so, the man decided that here was something significantly good that he could do. With all of his strength, he flipped the rock out of the way of the tree. With pride, he looked down at the cleared ground, and began to notice in shock that he had totally disrupted the lives of all of the small animals and creatures that had built their homes under that rock.

There is an expression 'Mind your own business.' People that take on responsibilities for others, especially tasks and duties that are not their responsibility, are often not minding their own business; they are often not taking care of themselves, and more often than they realize, they are disturbing the business of others.

I have observed the consequences of not minding your business in the corporate world. What often happens is that people, who take on the tasks of others, get more tasks. Because they are overworked, they are seldom seen by the people that make decisions over their promotion. Unfortunately, because they are supporting others, it is the others that prosper and advance instead of them. Take Phil, for example:

Phil was a programmer assigned to specialized research in a university department. Aside from being a programmer, he was also an expert with anything to do with computers. Many people, even from other departments would often go to him for help in repairing their own computer systems because everyone knew that if there was a solution, Phil would find it.

Although he was incredibly helpful, Phil was not very respected by his boss, and was constantly overlooked for promotion and funding. It may have been that his bosses simply took him for granted and knew that he could make do on a shoestring budget more easily than most. Out of eventual frustration, he moved on to another job somewhere else. After he left, of course, all of the computer systems, including the one Phil had used, had to be upgraded at considerable cost, in part, because nobody else could get the old systems to work. The irony of course, is that Phil and everyone else could have had much newer and better equipment from the beginning, if he were not so overly helpful to everyone else, and if he had minded his own business.

Many organizations fail or become less effective because a serious problem or issue is ignored too long if there is always someone around to patch over the situation or 'fix it.' The result can be very much like bad electrical wiring or plumbing that carries multiple temporary patches and fixes. Over time it can lead to disastrous consequences.

Sometimes, the serious problem involves personalities; people who are not doing their jobs or their behavior is interfering with the work of others. At these times, having someone come in and 'rescue' the situation may have the serious consequence of leaving an important issue hidden when it needs to be made visible or resolved as soon as possible.

People need acknowledgement and constructive criticism in order to grow and mature. People need to make mistakes and then learn from them. These processes can be interfered with, when people do not mind their own business.

We need to take responsibility for our own actions, and not steal that responsibility from others. If our actions come from a need to be helpful, we need to be careful, because much like that earlier story that the medicine man told, positive results often do not follow from neediness or 'good intentions.'

Some consequences of not minding your own business

Here is partial list to think about when it comes to minding your own business.

- People who are good at getting you to help them are often assessed as people who get things done. People who do things for them are often assessed as repair people or useful people. People that get things done are promoted. Useful people are kept where they are, because 'they are useful.'
- When you help someone who otherwise is not capable of doing it themselves, you bear some of the responsibility if they get promoted and you do not.
- You may have cheated someone out of their learning through trial and error, and through making mistakes on

their own.

- You may have cheated someone out of taking pride in their own accomplishment, so that they can say *"I did that!"*
- There may be a major flaw that needs to be corrected. The flaw could be in procedures, personnel or equipment, and your meddling may be preserving that flaw until it becomes a bigger problem.
- Your work suffers, and you may not get the recognition you desire. Employers usually don't find out or care if you are helpful to others. They care if your own productivity suffers.
- Who is minding your own business?

Whom are you parenting?

Often, people who are overly responsible can go to the extreme of mothering or fathering those around them. It is good to be someone who takes care of others, as the situation warrants it. What is not so good is to be so concerned about others that you are not taking care of yourself. The two situations often go hand in hand.

If you grew up in a household where you did not experience being nurtured, supported or taken care off, it may have left you with a sense of being unloved, hurt, unwanted or unvalued. Perhaps you noticed that your friends seemed to be getting that care and attention that you yourself craved.

Such experiences often make you much more sensitive to the needs of the people around you. You know what it is to be unsupported, and as a result, you now have a tendency to overly care for others.

If you do have a history of taking care of the needs of others, you tend to build up a lot of ability and skill. The trick is to take all of that ability and responsibility you have given away to others, and turn it around so that you can be your own best parent for your self! You can become someone who takes responsibility to protect your own feelings, your own needs and joy. It is never too late.

When you do this, the part of you that has been waiting to be taken care of all those years will finally receive the love and attention you crave and need. When you take care of your feelings, when you act as your own best parent, that part of you that has been holding back begins to feel safe, to feel more joy and aliveness. When this happens, you begin to trust being more alive. You begin to trust revealing more joy. This is when healing can take place. It begins by honoring yourself.

Are you honoring yourself?

Here are some questions to ask yourself in determining if you have a tendency not to take responsibility or to honor yourself:

- Do I make more promises than I can keep?
- Do I tend to promise to do things in the future as a way of pushing away responsibility in the present?
- Do I put off what I could do right now?
- Do I surround myself with obligations?
- Do I make time for myself?
- Am I constantly trying to keep up with yesterday?
- When I work with others, am I letting them off the hook more easily than myself?
- Am I taking care of myself?
- Do I take on responsibility without thinking or contemplating the consequences?
- Do I jump in when someone announces a problem or difficulty, with *"I can do that?"*
- Do I tend to have a list of things that I have obligated myself to do that leaves no room for anything that I want or need to do for myself?
- Do I avoid having a list of things to do for myself that I act on daily and that helps me move forward in life?

If you have answered yes to some of these questions, it is time to take your tendency to feel responsible for others and apply it towards being responsible for yourself. Begin by paying more attention to your feelings and needs, and take the time to consider your responsibilities to yourself, and to your heart, before you commit yourself to others. Honor yourself first!

Chapter Summary

We are responsible for our life, our actions and choices, because we bear the consequence. Ultimately we alone are responsible for our hearts, for honoring ourselves and our inner integrity. When we ignore our responsibility for ourselves, we are at risk for taking on the responsibilities of others in ways that do not benefit us. It is important that we notice when we do this. These are the very places in our lives that we need to refocus our effort to honor our heart and to take care of our feelings through appropriate actions.

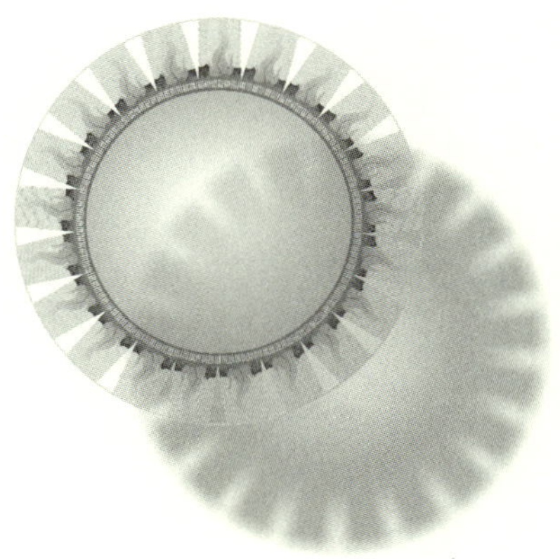

Addiction

What are you addicted to in your life?

Addiction may be described as a situation where you have entered into a dependent relationship with something outside of your self. It is something that brought relief or a heightened sense of joy at the beginning. Now, it negatively affects your life and you experience difficulty in letting go of this dependency.

Although we may have the impression that addiction is something removed from our lives, or that it happens to someone else, many of our behaviors, in one way or another, are addictions.

The wrong way home

Surprisingly, addiction occurs because we try to regain our center, our sense of joy and aliveness. It occurs because, in one way or another, we find ourselves identifying with being caught in a stance far removed from that joy, from that aliveness. We seek escape from being caught in our issues, and at the same time, we seek to taste some of that joy.

The problem for most of us is that when we choose an external agency to accomplish this, our joy or escape tends to be short lived. Often, we are brought back to where we started, except that we are brought back with a fall, a crash. Our escape did not solve our problem, it only postponed it. We may have gotten a taste of joy or expansion, but that taste came with a price.

That price was that we didn't achieve that experience out of ourselves, but out of an external agency. In a sense, we gave up a little of our will in exchange for a little bit of release from our burden. Unfortunately, we did not transform or solve the issue of where we were caught; we only postponed it. We still remain trapped as before, only now, we have a taste of what it is to feel more and to be able to flow in the moment.

At this point, some people rally to their experience and decide to do something positive with their lives, or with the situation that has them caught, because the glimpse of joy is enough to motivate them to make positive changes. They are willing to do the work to come closer to their core, to their joy, to who they truly are. They choose to return to their power. As a result, they choose not to enter into an addictive loop.

For others, the pull of something that gives them a glimpse of their own joy, or an escape from suffering, is too great. It is stronger than their willingness and ability to act to improve the situation they seek escape from. In a way, a growing addiction becomes a tug of war between tough love and easy love, between making an effort and procrastination. Eventually for these people, the identification shifts towards the agency that gives immediate relief, and an addictive pattern forms.

Because a little bit of the person's will has been given away in each return to the addiction, it becomes increasingly more difficult to let the addiction go and face the changes necessary to extricate oneself from the original problem. At each return, there is a demonstration of futility, of failure to succeed in stopping the process. The agent of addiction is the declared winner.

This situation is compounded by being pulled farther and farther away from one's core, with the result that as the addiction progresses one actually tends to feel less, and therefore must do more to get that glimpse of joy. For addictions to a substance (such as food, alcohol, cigarettes or drugs), this parallels needing to increase the amount of substance used, because the body builds up resistance.

An addicted person seeks a symbiotic relationship, a relationship they can win, but increasingly, this relationship becomes a dependant one. They identify with the agency of their addiction, but at each step of identification, the elusive agent still stays outside of their control. And so, they continually get pulled away from center. The solution lies in the other direction.

What makes addiction different?

How does addiction differ from simply being pulled away from our center? It differs because in addiction, we create a false center outside ourselves that temporarily mimics being connected to our heart or core. There is an artificial sense of being home. Often, there is an artificial sense of being in flow or being in the moment.

Early addictive experiences with gambling, shopping, eating, alcohol, drugs and other addictive patterns, often follow a pattern that starts out with pleasure, a sense of expansion or a freedom that is captivating. For some, there is the experience of states not normally encountered in their everyday lives. For others, the initial experience can be almost like worship. Some people's initial experiences with tobacco can be hallucinogenic, and at any time, nicotine can certainly be mind altering.

In many cases, some of the impetus for the addiction is in trying to recapture those initial experiences that seem like love-at-first-sight. Although we do what we can to stay 'in love', this unfortunately is a false love because it blinds us to our core. True love brings us closer to our heart and to our core.

As the addictive process continues, the attempt to recapture that expansion or pleasure is rewarded with decreasing success. In part, this is because the newness is gone or because our own body and 'energetics' have adapted. And of course, we are already less connected to our real center and own source of joy and flow.

In order to compensate, the pattern of increasing use begins, and with it the erosion of being centered and in the heart.

The cost of addiction

Addictions separate us from our support, family and friends. Addictions do this because our own connection to our core and to our heart is weakened. Our love for ourselves and for others becomes replaced by a false love towards the agency of the addiction, whether that agency is being a workaholic or an alcoholic.

Addictions waste our time. Instead of being alive for ourselves and doing the things that support our joy and aliveness, addictions devour our time and to varying degrees leave us lifeless if we allow it.

One of the real costs of addiction is that it uses up our own vitality, as its fuel. Often, that heightened sense of aliveness that we experience during addiction is the leaking, release and loss of our own energy and joy.

Imagine a bank robbery where some of the money accidentally spills out on the street. The bank manager, not being aware that a robbery is in progress, looks out the window and is all excited, because he thinks there is all of this extra money out there. He doesn't realize that what he is looking at is money that he is losing. For him, money is money. In addiction, it is the same; energy is energy. Energy leaking and being released from you feels just as good as energy that you are gaining or receiving. Unfortunately, you are robbing yourself! That is why, afterwards, your energy is down.

We can revel in the addictive experience as our vitality is released or bled, but afterwards we are confronted with the lowered state or low energy level that results. Now the cycle starts anew, as we seek escape from the very slump or fall that we created or participated in. With most addictions, the loss accumulates over time. Unfortunately, it often takes too long before we become aware of the extent of these losses and their effects on our lives. This is more than enough reason to break the addictive cycle before this happens.

Escaping from the escape of addiction

To escape from addiction, we need to begin to avoid the process of avoiding. We get caught in addiction because of two kinds of avoiding. The first is the tendency to not take responsibility for our lives or to not break the cycle of addiction that we may find ourselves in.

The second is the active creation of a 'void,' an emptiness that seeks something to fill it. That emptiness comes from disconnection from our core. Addictive behavior keeps plunging us back into that emptiness. In a sense, we need to avoid this void, by reconnecting to our hearts and to our core.

We need to begin to re-assert our will on an ongoing, daily basis in order to stop adding energy to our addictive process. This means facing the very issues that we tend to avoid, if necessary. This means healing some of our wounds which we avoid, or seek to cover up.

Many addictions are really extended platforms for our emotions. The rage of an alcoholic, the compulsion of a chain smoker, the 'high' a user may experience with some drugs, are often the play of the emotions that we hold back, or hold us back, under 'normal' circumstances. It is our emotions that are using us up for their own pleasure. What we do not receive from them is a re-connection to our core, to our heart. Yet, ironically, this is what we seek, but are caught up in reacting rather than acting. We are caught up in avoiding rather than becoming.

Reversing the process

The reversal of the process of addiction happens when we focus more energy towards our core and towards our feelings and towards being in the moment. Sometimes this happens when we are awakened by a shock, the slap of reality, or through Grace. It happens when we decide that enough is enough, when we take back our will and our responsibility.

In order to reverse addiction, we need to cut off the drag on our system that the addiction creates by re-asserting our will, even if one step at a time. We need to acknowledge ourselves each time we take a step, because acknowledging ourselves brings us closer to our core. We need to let ourselves know that our heart is still pure, that inside there is still joy and that we are on the right path. In a way, we need to parent ourselves because we are dealing with fundamental issues that we likely carried from childhood and those issues now need the loving and caring that we may not have received then.

Our feelings and reactions are really at a child-like level. When we told ourselves how bad we were in not being able to break with our addiction in the past, our system heard this. If we now acknowledge our successes, we hear this also. We partly become what we hear. Therefore, do not underestimate the power of self-acknowledgement.

In the next chapter are suggestions and guidelines for addressing addiction on a day to day basis. Be warned. You may say to yourself that you do not have addictions, that you do not need rehabilitation. But understand this. Addiction can gain ground with almost anyone, regardless of who or what they are, whether they think they are good people or not. It behooves you to at least look at the chapter from the point of being armed and ready. It is better to be prepared, than foolish.

> *Life is a process of becoming, a combination of states we have to go through. Where people fail is that they wish to elect a state and remain in it. This is a kind of death.*
>
> Anais Nin

Chapter Summary

In this chapter, we examined addictions from the perspective that they are artificial replacements for our connection to our heart and core. Addictions are maintained in part, because we give away our will to that replacement and in part, because the original void from which the addiction was a refuge, continues and is not healed. In order to overcome addiction, we need to strengthen the connection to our heart and our will.

Overcoming Addiction

The way that we lose our direction in life is by allowing ourselves to lose our connection to our center, to who we are. The journey back reverses that processes as we re-engage our intention, will and action.

The previous chapter introduced the basis of addiction from the point of view of our connection to our core. This chapter takes a more detailed look at what you can do about addiction. The tasks outlined in this chapter apply just as well to someone who has an addiction with attention seeking, overworking, food, spending, procrastination, substance abuse or any other addictive pattern.

The process of overcoming any addiction, often involves some or all of the following tasks. I have grouped these in order of immediacy or simplicity:

Foundation tasks

1. **Acknowledge that you have a problem**. Acknowledge there is a need to change and that you are willing to take action to make that change a reality. Often this impulse can occur as a result of a wake-up call.

2. **Acknowledge that you are greater than your problem.**

Acknowledge you are worth the effort to overcome your issue. You need to let yourself know that your worth cannot come from outside, that it resides inside you and always remains there, undiminished, no matter what.

3. **Become aware of your inner dialogue.** So many people put themselves down with inner criticism as a result of their addiction. Becoming aware of this dialogue will help you change or replace it. You must replace your self-criticism with words that strengthen your connection to your heart.

   Many people plot, with their thinking and awareness, how to maintain their addiction or how to keep it secret from others. It can become an automatic vigilance to maintain the resources for the addiction, even if all of the evidence shows that it is not doing them any good.

   You must replace your vigilance for the support of the addiction, with vigilance for the support of you. Catch yourself every time you put yourself down. As you do this, you become stronger; you will be strengthening your will and ability to overcome your addictive pattern.

4. **Become aware of your feelings.** Many people, when addicted are not aware of their feelings. Some even find it difficult to feel, and the closest thing to feeling, for them, becomes identified with the addictive behavior and the release or containment of emotion. It is important not to confuse feelings with emotions. Emotions have a charge to them and they hold un-integrated issues from the past. Addictive behavior, more often than not, relishes those emotions. In taking the path of emotions, a person depletes their energy, physically, emotionally and psychically, without getting any closer to healing their emotions.

   To heal, it is necessary to follow the path of feelings. Take the time to find out what you are feeling, especially at times when you are not sure what is going on. Acknowledge what you are feeling. This will help you reconnect with your heart. If you need more clarity, consider revisiting the chapter entitled *Feelings and Emotions*, earlier in this book.

5. **Become aware of your needs.** All too often, addiction compensates for needs that have not been met. There may be fear in asking for what you want, or there may be fear of leaving a situation in order to make what you need possible. In order to increase your success in overcoming addiction, find out what needs your addiction is allowing you to hide or substitute. Be mindful that what you want and what you need are not always the same. If you feel that your needs are reasonable be prepared to communicate, and if appropriate, to negotiate your needs.

Integration Tasks

6. **Learn to act from your heart.** A challenging event may have shocked you out of a complacency and awoken you to a state of being alive and real again. It may have even re-connected you to your heart again. This state shows you to be a person other than your addicted pattern. Don't lose this opportunity. Cultivate it. It is a gift and lifeline.

   In order to keep and maintain that gift of aliveness in your heart, you need to feed it; you need to tell yourself positive and encouraging things every time you do the right thing and you need to take care of your heart when you interact with others. Acting from your heart will bring an experience of more energy and joy, and this will lessen the tug of addiction away from the heart and will.

7. **Learn to notice and make changes.** What do you see yourself doing over and over again? Do you see yourself becoming more of a recluse, or less effective as a result of your addiction? What positive changes could you make to help yourself? What are you going to do about it? Write out the steps necessary to be successful in making changes. Where do you need to start? What do you need to change? What trips you up? Who trips you up? What can you do to improve the situation? Then, start making changes.

8. **Are you neglecting yourself?** Are you making others more important than you, and compensating for this with your addiction? Are you living your life for others to the extent that your addiction is your effort to regain something for yourself? Have you made yourself important in your life? Are you taking care of your feelings, your wishes, goals and aspirations, or are you following the needs of others?

   You must have a meaningful relationship with your own best interests and with your own heart. If you are pulled to relate to the needs of others instead of your own, you are likely to seek a crutch to lean on for your own needs in order to sustain this choice.

   It is an age old adage: if you don't love yourself, you really can't love someone else. The corollary here is that when you try to love someone else before you have learned to love yourself, you may end up depleting yourself and disconnecting from your heart. When you are dry inside, you go through the motions of living without being alive, and gather crutches and addictions to sustain you. To get rid of these crutches, begin by regaining and honoring your own heart.

9. **Are you acting for your self?** Where have you given your power away? Do you take care of the feelings of others, but not your own? Are you overly nice to others, and not so nice to yourself? Is your addiction a compensation for this? Are you hiding your true feelings, responses and needs, in order to be liked or loved? Do you feel that there is something dark or unlovable about you that compels you to hold back your spontaneity and openness with others? Do you seek your addiction to give you that sense of being alive? Is it really giving you that, or simply holding you? What is it that you need to accept about yourself in order to free your joy? Is your addiction being used to support a contracted sense of who you are?

10. **What do you need to let go of?** Are you holding on to material things or mementos that have no other purpose but to

remind you to suffer? Have you allowed things simply to accumulate to the point that they constrict the energy and space in which you live? It may be time to let go of these things if their only purpose now is to pull you down.

Moving forward

11. **Trust.** Trust that you can do it. Trust that you are greater than what you have gotten stuck in, and trust that it does not define you. Trust that if you make the effort, the universe will support you. Trust that your life will improve once you let go of what is holding you back.

    Trust in yourself grows as you take those actions that bring you closer to your heart. Trust with others grows when you do those things that prove to yourself that you can be more alive as you are, that you honor your feelings and that you are willing to appropriately take care of yourself. As your trust grows, so do you.

12. **Take responsibility.** Make sure that you are taking care of your feelings before you take care of others; that you are taking care of your own business before you take care of other people's business, and that you are focusing on your goals before you focus on the goals of others. When you don't mind your own business, when you don't take care of yourself and your needs, don't be surprised if you start trying to compensate with addictive behavior. And, if you have chosen to get past an addiction, draw up your battle plan and draw your boundaries. Fight to determine who is the boss — you or your addiction. Begin to administrate your life. Make the effort and focus on the goal. Honor your effort and honor yourself.

13. **Become open to change.** Take a course, a workshop, or start a new hobby. Go out and meet new friends. Move around the furniture, or try out new ways to rearrange the familiar things around you. Let go of unneeded items that surround you, at home and at work. Outward changes help trigger and

support inner ones.

14. **Reconnect with your spirit and soul.** Do things that give you a sense of awe, wonder and joy, on a regular basis. For some people, it can be music or art. For others, being at the park, the woods or nature brings them back to a sense of stillness. Yoga, meditation and other practices of various spiritual traditions can help to connect you to your essence. Do what connects you to the moment. It is all that there really is.

15. **Find a passion.** More often than not, an addictive cycle indicates that, in at least one aspect of your life, you have been experiencing a lack of passion. Get out and meet people. Go to workshops. Get involved. Ask for what you want or need. Find something to look forward to. It is very important to replace the vacuum that the addiction may be trying to fill. Fill it with something else.

16. **Choose a physical activity.** When you move your body, when you exercise, you increase your vitality, you raise your endorphin levels which results in feeling better, and you dissipate some of the negative energy that may be clinging to you. It is a good idea to develop a regular exercise program, even if it is simply walking daily.

17. **Clear your immediate environment.** The way you keep your place of residence, the way you put things away or just let them pile up, quite literally declares your inner state. If you are procrastinating, then more often than not, you let things pile up. If you are caught up in an addictive syndrome, then you tend to neglect how your surroundings look.

    Your state has a profound effect on your immediate environment. However, it also works both ways; your environment has a profound effect on you. If the sky is muggy and dark, you tend to feel it, and when the sun comes out, there tends to be a rise in spirits. In the same way, if you have created a mess around you, then that mess will affect you. If you clear up that mess, if you keep your areas organized, then that will affect you also. Therefore, make the effort to clear the energy of your immediate environment regularly, because it will be a way of clearing yourself!

Your body also tends to hold negative energies, and it is important to clear these also. Taking regular showers with the intension to remove these residues is one of the easiest and simplest ways to clear.

In addition to clearing your surroundings and body, make sure that you clear your mind and your thoughts. As negative thoughts and ideas arise, replace them with positive ones. If you find yourself putting yourself down, start examining ways that you have been good, successful, and positive. Acknowledge yourself for each thing you did or said that moved you forward. Acknowledge yourself for making the effort to move forward now. The secret to clearing old, damaging and useless thoughts about yourself is to replace them with positive, supportive and healing thoughts. Each positive thought is like a little shower that helps clear away the debris of negative thought. Develop this habit of clearing. Do it with intention and it will have a profound effect on your life.

18. **Avoid the pitfalls.** Become aware of the patterns and situations that tend to result in addictive relapse. For example, some people with food addictions are fine until the evenings, when they begin to crave. They need to acknowledge that crave phase honestly and replace it with something else: going to bed earlier, making tea, having a glass of water or having food available that is more acceptable.

    The trick is to find alternative positive actions that allow you to get past that craving successfully. Some people may find that they are successful on their own, but tend to fail when they are with others or in social company. For them, solid alternative choices and plans of action need to be readied in advance, like actually bringing safe food or snacks they can eat in company, or making sure they have access to these alternatives. Sometimes, it can help to let everyone know your intentions and even ask for their support so that you can get past old habits in social situations.

You have to be honest with yourself: until you are strong enough to avoid losing ground with your friends, you may have to choose your company well.

Additional factors in overcoming addictions

There are several additional factors that are key in overcoming addictions:

1. **A strong willingness to change.** You need a willingness to change and make a one hundred percent effort. So many people are willing to change but place too much of the responsibility on others. You have to make the change your priority. You have to make your self and your life a priority. Not being one hundred percent committed tends to drag out various forms of intervention, such as counseling and therapy, past their usefulness. In fact, people waste great sums of money going to sessions that become crutches that drag out change. These ultimately support their bad patterns. Don't fall into this trap. If you are one hundred percent committed, the universe will come to your aid. If you are ninety nine percent committed, the universe will conspire with you to delay due to that one percent.
2. **A strong intention to change.** Some people shop around for help, but never stop shopping because their intention is not clear and focused on making a positive change. You might look at your willingness as an engine, and your intention as your steering wheel. Although you may be very willing and desirous of change, unless you set your sights directly on change, you are at risk of being swayed from your goal. Be clear what your goal is. Be clear what it is that you need to do. The steering wheel is in your hands; therefore, steer towards solutions and success and stay on that road.
3. **A willingness to bounce back.** It is too tempting for many

people to simply give up when they fail to reach their goal the first time, or when they trip up. For some, it is an excuse they give themselves and others *"I tried, really, I tried."* Now they can dive into their addiction without having to hold back. Without a doubt, giving up an addiction is a struggle both on the inside and on the outside. And that struggle often extends to your environment, friends and family. You have to see the larger picture as it may take several steps. Take the time to envision all of the steps realistically. In order to bounce back, be willing to attack the issue, in steps that you can handle. If you fall, that's Okay. Get up, shake yourself off and move on! We all learn from our falls. We become stronger until we succeed.

4. **Overcome blame.** When you fall, the danger is to blame yourself. Blaming yourself will only decrease your energy, reinforce your experience as a failure, and make what you are trying to let go of bigger than you are. In reality, blame is making something else or someone else responsible for your choices and hence the outcome. Instead, become your own coach. Pat yourself on the back for making an effort, and then give yourself a kick start to make it successful. Find out why you were not successful. Make the necessary changes. People, who fail to overcome their addiction to sweets on their very first try, need to get rid of their candies, cookies and sweets in the house, ask their family to co-operate, restock the house with alternatives, and then try again. This is a better choice than blaming the sweets, their family or their lack of will. Each time you take responsibility for your actions and their outcomes, and avoid blaming, you make a stronger showing and you lessen the hold of your addiction, until you succeed.

5. **Take action in the direction of change.** Just setting a date to begin getting rid of an addiction doesn't usually work. You have to be willing and able to put out the effort and then do it! Do something that makes the addiction weaker in relationship to you. Get rid of the things that anchor the

addiction. If you have a food addiction, then throw out and replace the food you are addicted to with food that is better for you. Every action that you choose that strengthens you in relation to an addiction will help shift the balance in your favor. But you have to begin doing these actions. Demonstrate to yourself that you are greater than your addiction. If you are getting rid of an addictive pattern, consider consciously replacing that pattern with something else.

6. **Heed the wake up call.** Some people let their addiction drift until they get a wake up call — a situation or event that forces them to reconsider where they are going. The pivoting point can be reaching rock bottom and realizing that their very life is in their hands. For others, it can be an event that forces them to take a hard look at themselves.

   Don't ignore your wake up call. Choose a pivoting point in your life, or have it choose you. Either way, the consequences of your actions related to addiction have created a crisis that needs your immediate attention. That wake up call shocks you towards your core, your heart, your center. You can make an effort from within you, rather than from the place of attachment. Take the call; seize your life.

7. **Change your environment.** An exciting new adventure, meeting new friends or a positive change in your surroundings can help bring you back to life, and support you in giving up a bad habit or addiction. It is important to take responsibility for the change in your life. If you change for others in order to seek approval, meet other's expectations, or bend to pressure, you put yourself at risk that the addiction may return as soon as you feel abandoned or rejected by those you sought to please. Take the opportunity, but make the change for yourself.

8. **Be honest with yourself.** Are you truly willing to give up your addiction and its consequences? Often an addiction is a crutch to survive something else that is more emotionally or physically threatening than the addiction. Perhaps it is

a bad relationship. Perhaps it is an avoidance of a painful action or responsibility. Whatever underlies your addiction also undermines your attempts to change. You must resolve this issue if you seek success with overcoming an addiction. Otherwise, the addiction is just a bandage to a wound. Each time you try to remove the bandage you are forced to replace it, and so, not only does the addiction return, but your self-confidence lessens.

9. **Change your stance with others.** Although you have made the effort to change, the people around you, your friends and family, may still hold the patterns that pull you back, or may still hold the image of your old way of being. Be prepared for this. Many people re-kindle their addictions as they rejoin their drinking buddies, addicted friends, etc. You have to decide where to draw the line. You have to ask yourself if being with the 'boys' or the 'girls' is more important than the effort and commitment you have made to yourself. Don't be surprised if some of your buddies were never your friends, but co-conspirators in your addiction. Some may actually work against you as you try to heal or regain your will. In a way, this is where you really find out who your true friends are.

10. **Heal the wound holding the addiction.** In order to stabilize the change you have made, it helps to confront the wound that may have gotten you addicted. Often negative feelings and avoidances tend to foster addictions. If you tend to over-eat because you are filling a vacuum of loneliness or lack of fun in your life then do something that lifts you out of that state. If you are in a relationship, make an effort to ask for what you need. If you seek relationship, get yourself into some activities, workshops or classes that place you with the type of people you want to attract. You have to do these actions if you want changes to occur. In this way, you let the universe know you are open to expansion, to receiving.

11. **Open your heart.** Addiction takes root when you are avoiding

being in the moment, being who you truly are. It occurs in disconnection from the heart, and maintains that disconnection. To break away from this cycle, do the things that reconnect you to your heart, to your own joy and openness.

> *Turn your face to the sun*
> *and the shadows fall behind you.*
>
> Maori proverb

Chapter Summary

In this chapter, we examined the process of letting go of addiction, by acknowledging the extent of the problem and acknowledging your worth, inner dialogue, feelings and needs. We looked at action from the heart, trust and responsibility and what we need to do to replace addiction with something more meaningful in our lives.

In addition to making any effort, we looked at important factors we need to confront in order to make the effort more successful. These include our honesty, willingness, intention and resilience. Some of the patterns that hold addiction through others need to be addressed. We need to face own relationship with our heart and the wounds we carry.

Overcoming addiction is really about coming home to the integrity of feelings and of being centered and in the heart. For this reason, your inner home must become more alive, meaningful and greater than the artificial home that has taken so much focus.

Taking Care of What You Hold in Your Heart

What have you chosen to worship?

Whatever we place in our hearts can have power, because we give it our will. We treasure what is in our hearts, whether it is true or not true, whether it is beneficial for us or pulls us down. Here we identify at a deep level, and so this affects not only our feelings and self image, but also what we are open to in life and what we feel is not open to us.

We treasure and worship what we hold in our hearts. Not only do we ourselves respond to what is in our hearts but life and the people around us respond also. In this way, whether we are conscious of it or not, we attract to ourselves our experiences that are in tune with what we worship and give power in our hearts. This is how we manifest our experiences and our destiny. Take care of what you hold in your heart.

Smiling parents

I once met someone who related to me an astounding discovery. For years he kept a vision of his parents as he had experienced them, with their criticism, disapproval and lack of warmth.

These were the personal images he held about his parents. Close to his heart, he gave these images power, even over himself.

He later decided to replace these images with ones that he wanted, of parents that smiled at him, that were loving, open, warm and encouraging to him. Every time he reflected upon his parents, or a recollection or mention of them happened, he would bring himself back to these positive images that he had placed in his heart. This is all he did — he replaced the images of his parents in his heart.

He related to me how, over a span of only a few days, his real parents seemed more loving, more open and more welcoming! He himself had also become more open. It was not just his impression of them that had changed. They really did behave more lovingly towards him. They did in fact become more like the images he held of them in his heart!

What we hold in our hearts, we worship. Be careful what you worship. Catch yourself when you find yourself worshiping beliefs and images about yourself that limit you or that put you down. Replace them with images that connect you to your positive qualities, your strengths and values and what you have to offer.

Positive images, especially the ones you place in your heart, have great power to transform you because they align you to a vision of your self and of others that is deeper than words, criticism or judgment. They can pull you towards alignment with your center, and they can also pull you to be in greater alignment with others.

An exercise

Consider trying this exercise. Ask yourself, what is in the image that you keep in your heart of the most important people in your life? What do the images look like? Are the people smiling, frowning, encouraging or critical? What are they saying? What is your response to the images? If it helps you, make a sketch and jot down the main remarks.

Once you have done this and after you have read the next

paragraph, sit in a comfortable posture for a few minutes and close your eyes:

Begin with the person that affects you the most. What is the image of this person that you wish was there? What do they look like? What are they saying? How do you respond to them? What is your experience of them and of yourself with the new image? Now, imagine that you are placing this image in your heart to replace the ones you have been holding. Consider it an installation ceremony. Repeat this same process with other important people in your life.

At least once a day, for the next few days, make an effort to re-install these images over the old ones. After a few days, check to see how you are doing: Do you notice any changes? Do you need to revise or renew the images? Many people are surprised at how easy and effective this process can be. This process may take a couple of weeks to take hold, so take care to reserve your judgments until you have made the effort.

An enemy, a friend

A long time ago, I had to work with a technician who was very opinionated and uncompromising. Everyone had difficulty with him. It turned out that he had been a political refugee and a former military officer. He was used to giving out orders, some quite harsh. He was not used to being a technician or getting along with people. Unfortunately, I could not avoid him, because we often had to work together.

One day, I decided to find a way to cut through the bad energy that was mounting between us, so I decided to try an experiment. I decided to act as if he were the opposite of how he was. I began to think positive thoughts in his direction. I took the most positive interpretation of his actions. I acted as if we were on good terms. I, in fact, installed a vision of him in my heart that was kind, generous and open minded. I did this as a disciplined exercise. Whenever we interacted, I responded to him from this image in my heart. He continued to be as he was, but I responded from this image that I now held of him.

The situation between us improved, markedly. In less than two weeks the tension and frustration, at least for me, had greatly diminished. After about two years, he retired. I met him passing on the street soon after, and he stopped, and grabbed my arm. He said *"I must tell you that of all of the people I worked with, you were truly like my son."* We had connected deeply because I had decided to hold his positive image in my heart. His heart picked it up. That is how hearts are, so notice what you hold in yours.

Do you hold yourself in your heart?

What is the image that you hold of yourself in your own heart? Is the image of yourself in your own heart someone who is loved and worthy of being loved? Is it an image of someone who is successful, a good person, someone who appreciates her own worth and will stand up for herself and for the right choices? Or, do you hold an image of yourself that is never good enough, that is afraid of success, of closeness or of receiving appreciation from others? Do you hold and image of yourself still waiting for your parents to tell you that you are loved, that you are a good son or daughter?

There is no reason to hold a negative image of yourself in your own heart. What do you think you will gain by doing so? A negative image will only attract negative things. Is this what you want? Regardless of what has happened to you, holding a negative image will not get you what you need: the spontaneity of your own heart, the joy of being in the moment, of being fully alive and the courage that shines out of your own heart. The negative images that you place in your heart hide these qualities. So try an experiment to change these for the better. What can you lose, except some of the ways that you hold yourself back?

Exercise two

Take the time to contemplate and identify what you hold about yourself in your own heart. Imagine what you looked like growing up. Imagine what your face looked like. How did you hold your body? What were some of the negative beliefs about yourself that you held in your heart at that time? Are you still holding any of these beliefs or images about yourself now? Close your eyes for a minute or two to contemplate these images.

Now, recall some of the times when you were happy, joyful, and alive. Try to recall times and events in your life when you were feeling loved, appreciated, and powerful. Was there a time when your heart was so full of joy that it almost felt like it was going to burst? How did you feel? Can you remember times when things just flowed, when everything just seemed right? How did it feel to be you then? Close your eyes again as you contemplate this.

Relax your breath. Take deep comfortable breaths.

Imagine that the images that you have been holding of yourself, that put you down, that held you back, that held pain and separation, are gently floating away with each out breath. Let it be so. These images were never really you.

As you breathe in, place those good times, those memories of joy and love into your heart, so that you can have access to this joy and love any time that you want or need.

As you breathe out, breathe out the images of disconnection, separation and fear.

Breathe in the images of joy, connection and love.

Don't force your breath, just be aware of the process. Give life to the images that are peak experiences for you, experiences of heartfulness and fullness. Close your eyes and continue this process for a few minutes. Do this now. (Take as long as you need.)

From now on, become aware of the images that you have placed in your heart. Each day, for the next few days, remind yourself, in a way meaningful to you that these images of your own love for yourself are in your heart. Access them. It is best to do this when you wake up, at the beginning of your day. Do it also at other times, when you remember, when you interact with others, before important meetings, or where you have to present yourself. Do it as you go to sleep.

After several days, or a week or two, check to see how you

are doing. Did you notice any changes? Did you notice a positive shift, even if it was subtle at first?

You can continue to hold negative images of yourself if you wish. Or, you can let them go. You can also hold positive experiences and images of yourself in your heart. The effects of what you hold in your heart are very powerful. The choice is yours.

Exercise three

Along with the images in our hearts, we also keep a sense of who we are, in terms of qualities. We may hold qualities that we may not like. We may yearn for personal qualities we wish we had. The qualities that we hold and those that we yearn for also tend to define us.

Let's try another experiment. Choose a quality that you would like to encourage in yourself. Perhaps that quality is strength, steadfastness, self-respect or courage. If at first a quality does not come up, contemplate what quality you admire in others. Write down this quality on a piece of paper. Buy and gift yourself a flower. Place the flower in a vase or glass and place the vase on top of your piece of paper.

We are going to honor this quality, and your heart, through the gift of the flower. Giving, when it is genuine, is always a two way process. In giving, we also open to receiving. It is really about gratitude.

Offer the written quality to your own heart. Let your heart receive this quality. Be at ease, as you imagine that you are placing this quality in your heart. If you wish, close your eyes and imagine this quality entering you and settling in your heart. Know that this quality is in you.

For the next few days, let the flower remind you of the quality that you welcomed into your heart. Take the time to acknowledge that you have welcomed this quality and take the time to receive it fully. Let that quality grow in your heart for you. Nurture it. Take care of it. Recognize it. Let it blossom like a flower.

Take care what you hold in your heart

Whatever we hold in our heart becomes real for us. It becomes not only what we believe about ourselves and others, but also, what we end up worshipping and manifesting in our lives. Therefore, take great care what you place in your heart and also what you let other people place there.

Become a good gardener in your heart. Take out the weeds that do not belong there. Take out all the limiting images and perceptions that you no longer need to carry. Start planting good seeds that bear good fruits. Acknowledge your good qualities; nurture and encourage these and new ones. Become a loving and caring gardener towards yourself and your own heart and you will be rewarded with a great heart. Your inner garden will flourish, and you will be more and more drawn to spend time there, to relax and bask in the freedom of your own heart. You will be more drawn to the joy that you have welcomed there. Take care what you place in your heart.

Chapter Summary

In this chapter, we have examined the power and effect of the images and qualities that we keep in our hearts. We can choose what we hold in our hearts. We can affect changes in ourselves and in our relationship with others by being conscious of what we allow to be held in our heart.

Grace

We often talk about the experience of grace as if it is something that happens to us, from the outside. Grace exists in our openness to what is being offered, on the inside and the outside. Grace is all around us in everything, in all actions and experiences. It is only our contracted sense of who we are, and what we are worthy of receiving, that limits our experience of what is offered.

I once participated in a three day hatha yoga workshop. I knew that it would be intense, a kind of physical boot camp for the heart and soul, and a very real test of my fitness, strength and flexibility. For several weeks, I prepared myself and diligently worked on my stretches and endurance. Yet, in the first ten minutes of the much anticipated workshop, I managed to pull the muscles in my right shoulder, and then twist my left wrist!

What happened, what was going on? Did the universe want me to stay out of shape? It was a blow to my ego, a painful one at that. I had to step back and assess the situation to find that I had pushed myself. I had entered the workshop trying to prove something, rather than being open to the teachings and instruction that was being offered. I had paid a lot for this workshop, so I had no intention of backing out.

My first lesson was to learn to listen to my own body, to be very conscious of each muscle. In order to function with these injuries, I had to draw on everything I had learned. I had to stay absolutely focused and conscious of my body, to compensate with what was working, and to relax and protect the areas of injury. As long as I was very aware and one-pointed all of the time, I learned that I could do handstands and support my weight, after a fairly short time. With all of the stretching, by the third day, the injuries were no longer a concern. They had forced me to be so tuned to my body, that I came out of the workshop transformed. I had made astounding progress, and I became grateful for the learning and transforming opportunity my temporary physical limitation had given me!

The key, on hindsight, was that I became open to what I was receiving, moment to moment. There was grace in the injury, even if it was so disappointing and even outrageous at the beginning. I was open to the gift, and the grace that it bestowed. This is what grace can be like. We want grace to appear according to our will, or to our limited view of what we need or want. Grace happens when we don't put up walls and expectations. It happens when we open to what is offered.

Grace and flow

We often associate grace with the arts. We experience dance as graceful because it expresses movement in such a way that each step, each movement, however difficult, flows. The dancer, through practice and sacrifice makes themselves an instrument of that flow. It is the ability to communicate that experience of flow to the audience that establishes this as an art.

We sometimes forget that art has its ancient roots in the spiritual, and that only in modern times we see art for art's sake. It is the ability to bring us into the moment, into flow and into our hearts that makes art truly worthwhile. In this way, art is a vehicle of grace, of connecting us to the experience of the gift in each moment.

The performing arts have an added advantage as vehicles of grace — the heart and state of the performer.

Sometimes you hear a musician who is technically a genius, yet, you feel no joy, no soul and no aliveness in what they do. What comes out is just technique, just control.

Other times, you might hear a musician less technically skilled, yet when they play something happens that reaches the audience and transforms them. What is going on? The performer has connected to their heart, and through that connection they also connect to the hearts of the audience. At some point, the performer surrendered to the moment, to flow, to the freedom of the expression of their heart, to the courage of the moment, to grace. They risked being in the moment and encouraged the audience to take that leap with them. Grace descended and magic happened! This same magic is available in our daily lives, once we are willing to take the leap toward the moment, towards grace.

Will and willingness

How we own our will determines our relationship with grace. When we give our will away, we also give away our ability to take in grace.

When we give will away, we do so in one of two ways. We make others responsible in our lives for what we experience and in this way we blame them for our issues. This is one way we give away our will, and push away our openness to grace.

Another way is through **willfulness**. We relate willfulness with being unreasonably stubborn or headstrong. The mind uses 'will' when disconnected from the heart. This kind of will is controlling and contracts our openness to receiving. It swims against the current of what the universe offers us. It therefore works against grace and luck.

The process of taking back our will takes us in the direction of reconnecting with our hearts. The kind of will that comes from re-connection to the heart is welcoming. It is cheerful, supportive and ready. It is **'willing'** and open to going with the flow that the universe offers us. It therefore works with grace and luck. In fact willingness welcomes these into our lives.

Being open to grace

How does one open to grace? You start by valuing yourself. Too many people when they seek grace, come with too small a cup. There is the expression, 'seek and you shall receive'. Often people seek grace in a contracted state and are surprised when they receive a contracted experience of grace. Yet, this is how the universe works.

To become truly open to grace, you have to become truly open to who you are, to your own greatness and to your own worth. You have to protect your worth, from those people whom you allow to take it from you and from the past impressions and issues that may have contracted your sense of worth.

The act of truly being open to grace arises from the stance of gratitude. When we fully embody gratitude, we value what we receive, we value who we are and we value the source and process of receiving. Gratitude opens the heart and makes our cup greater as we resonate with receiving. In response, the universe is delighted to fill our cup. This is how the universe is.

Grace is not about analyzing or logic. Grace takes the path of the heart, of unity, trust and faith. Grace happens when we are willing to be open in our hearts. In a way, it is our expansion of our heart, both inwardly to ourselves and to our core and outwardly towards others and to the universe, that opens us to grace.

Luck

Many people equate grace with luck. Although they are related, they are quite different. Simply put, grace opens you up to receiving on the inside, and luck opens you up to receiving on the outside. Luck happens when we are willing to be greater, when we are willing to seek expansiveness, and when we are willing to be open to a positive future.

In many spiritual traditions, luck is an attribute of merit, of having accumulated the dues to be worthy of receiving positive experiences or rewards. You get the sense that something is going on, because some people just seem to be lucky!

For most of us, luck is actually present in countless ways, but we may not be as open to it as we might wish. It has been my observation, that those who consider themselves unlucky are often also the ones that have difficulty receiving or accepting what is being offered to them. One wonders if an experience caused the avoidance in receiving, or whether it was the avoidance itself that brought about the experience. Often, the two are linked.

People with a more positive outlook about themselves, that are more open to what life has to offer, tend to notice the benefits that come their way. There is the expression, "*You make your own luck.*" Part of the meaning here is that you have to do the work that prepares the way for success. It also means that the preparation includes creating the stance, the intention and the openness to receiving what may be offered. This welcomes and attracts luck. Last, but not least, is the willingness to notice the luck that comes your way and to do something about it!

There is another expression 'beginners luck' which may be true. There is of course a trick. The trick is that beginners usually approach things from a more open perspective than one who has experience or seems to know what they are doing. The problem with having your perceptions clouded with experience is that you begin to see and notice only what you think is there. You start to put 'blinders' on.

If you wish to increase your luck, do the things that bring you closer to being alive, to being in your feelings and in your heart. Practice being in the moment, being present and being aware. Practice using your will and your freedom to creatively think out of the box, and let go of the useless false beliefs about yourself that hold you back.

When you risk being more present and expanded, when you greet the world with fresh eyes, the luck around you becomes crystal clear. Then you are open enough to the gifts that come your way to acknowledge them and apply them to your life.

Ways to increase your luck and openness to grace

Here are some tips for increasing your chances of benefiting from the luck and grace that comes your way:

- When something good happens to you, acknowledge it and thank the universe for what you receive. Be grateful. As your heart opens to receive and acknowledge, it opens to receive even more. So be 'great-full.' Be willing to be full and to be fully open.

- Some people say grace when they eat. It is very beneficial to have a thankful stance towards the offering of food before eating. In this way, you practice opening your heart in thanks, and in your willingness to receive what is offered, not just with food, but with all of the experiences that sustain and feed you in your life.

- Don't expect things to be exactly the way you want. Often, waiting for things to be perfect is a way to delay receiving what is offered. It is far easier to find the gems that life offers and honor them, than to wait forever for something that must fulfill your expectations. You must give grace at least a little elbow room. If you don't give grace some space to enter your life, then, where do you imagine it is going to appear?

- When your luck seems to be down for a period of time, consider the possibility that the universe is trying to tell you something. What is it that you need to change in yourself, or in the way you interact, for your luck to improve?

- Think positive thoughts. Catch yourself when putting yourself down. Do positive actions. Acknowledge the good things that you do. As you increase the resonance to grace and luck in yourself, grace and luck are drawn towards you.

Chapter Summary

In this chapter we looked at grace and luck from the point of view that we are actually surrounded by these in our lives. The reason we do not experience as much of these as we wish is that we tend not to be open or aware of what is offered us because we hold the belief that we are not worthy or it comes in ways that we do not expect, appreciate or welcome. In order to bring more grace and luck into our lives, we need to honor these as we receive them. We can do this by validating the gifts that come our way and we can validate ourselves through our own worthiness to receive.

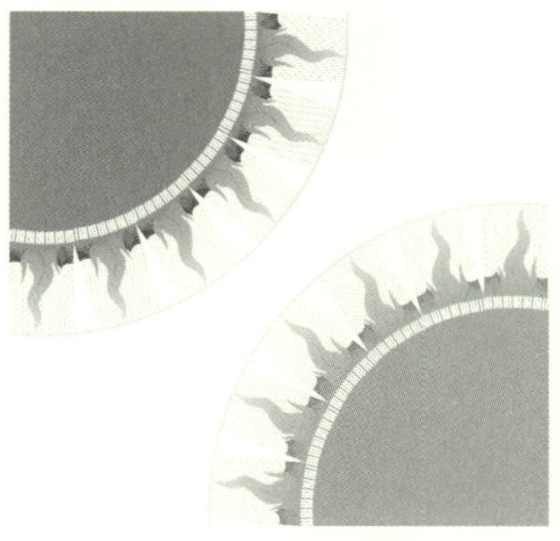

Seeking Advice

Many people, at one time or another, seek advice or begin a longer process of transformation with the help of someone who is skilled and who has made that journey themselves. I have not found much, already written, to help people in their search for such guidance, so I have included some advice here.

As silly as it sounds, you would not go to a bricklayer to paint your office, or a landscaper to fix your plumbing, yet people often seek help in a time of crisis or transition without determining if they are choosing the right type of coach, counselor or practitioner. It is important to figure out, at least in a general way, what it is that you need.

Once you have a clearer sense of what you need to do and what advice or support will help you, then, you will be starting out on the right foot. In this way, the advice takes you forward and you can know whether it is beneficial for you, whether it works for you and whether it is something that you need. Otherwise, you risk being pulled away from what you need and pulled towards what other people think you need.

Preparing yourself

Before you seek advice, it is helpful to prepare yourself for receiving advice. Contemplate what it is that you are seeking. It may help going for a walk to give yourself time to figure out what is troubling you, or what you are searching for. If you can, determine what is not working for you and what a solution to your issue may look like. Get a sense of your present situation and of where you may need to go.

If you do not know where to start, the next sections will help you begin this process.

Three steps

The first step is to listen to your heart and determine what it is you are feeling and what your heart is telling you. From knowing what is in your heart, comes clarity and openness to receiving the advice offered. It can also protect you from having yourself pulled away from your own best interests.

Of course, at times it may be difficult to figure out what is in your heart if your emotions and reactions are at play. In this case, someone you trust can help identify what you really want, where your feelings lie, and what it may be that you need. Remember that you are seeking your own clarity, so continue to check what is in your heart and what it is that you need. The process of seeking advice is best when it supports you in knowing what is in your heart and takes you towards effective outward action.

The second step in seeking advice is to listen, without judgment or interference, to the advice you are being given. You cannot receive advice unless you are open to listening.

The third step is to test what you have received against what your heart feels is appropriate for you. Does the advice move you forward? Does it feel good? Does the advice truly move you towards freedom? What are you gaining? What are you losing? Is your inner child happy with the new directions? Also, assess the consequences and the effect of the proposed changes — are they beneficial? Check to see if the advice received is supporting taking responsibility or giving it away, taking power or giving it away.

After you have prepared yourself and found that the advice is beneficial, are you ready to act on it? What is holding you back?

Choosing the right means

In order to move forward, in order to let go of what holds you back, it is important to keep checking that the methods you choose aren't sabotaging the process and returning you towards being stuck all over again. This is very important.

Often, people who are ready to move forward feel raw and vulnerable, and they may not be in the best circumstances from which to choose the directions and offerings most beneficial for them. There are many support systems, some costly, that provide varying returns for the effort. Some actually can set you back, because they steal the opportunity for your healing had you chosen the right means in the first place. It is important that you find a process that fits your needs and that will help your growth, rather than wasting your time and energy adapting to a process.

It is therefore important to choose wisely. For starters, get second opinions. If you are contemplating starting a long series of sessions with someone, first try out three different people, in order to evaluate whom you trust and who seems to offer what you need.

Consider spending a tenth of the total amount set aside for your healing on finding the right person. Often, this can save you a great deal of money, time and effort. More importantly, it can save the opportunity to move forward. Do not get caught in the trap of feeling obligated in continuing with someone only because you have already started with him. In fact, if you feel caught, that of itself may be a message for you to rethink your choice.

Consider making three appointments with three different counselors. It may be possible to schedule three short and free evaluative interviews – find out. The more you find out at the very beginning, the further ahead you will soon be. After evaluating each counselor, you are likely to be in a better position to make up your mind as to which one better fits your needs.

Here are some things to consider as you start out. Later, you may want to see how these apply to your sessions:

1. **Have you chosen the right process?** It is important that you find a process that fits your needs, rather than wasting time and energy fitting yourself to a process. Many techniques and skills are available that parallel different stages and needs for your growth. Find out early if the process you are starting is working for you. If not, inquire what is available that is closer to what you need.

2. **In your heart, do you trust this person?** Is she reaching out to you from her heart? Do you sense or feel that she presents herself as she is, with integrity and honesty, or, is she hiding behind technique, professionalism or rules? If you don't trust her now, how will you be able to trust her with your deepest feelings later in the process?

3. **Does this person have courage?** Is she capable and willing to go with you to the depths of your issue and help you move forward, or is she hiding behind rules, technique and methodology. Do you sense she has moved through her own issues? Has she solved her own problems? If someone you have chosen to help you is afraid of going past where you need help, then how is she going to help you?

4. **Is this person asking you to adapt?** Adapting is not the same as moving forward and it can more likely be a setback. This can be the case if your progress is measured by how much you have adapted to a system or set of techniques. Trust your heart. Trust your own sense of whether you are making progress with these techniques or whether you need to go elsewhere.

5. **Does the counselor seem to be integrated as a person?** Often, when people come from their core or center they are

effective and tend not to push your buttons. They are clear and direct. They manifest no sense of neediness or control.

6. **Is there a two-way exchange of power?** The counselor is sharing her will and courage with you because you need support. What are the indications that she has your best interests at heart? Is she willing, able and likely to help support the healing of your will and courage? Ideally, you are not to be dependent on her at the end of the process. Is she willing to support your self-independence or is she making you dependent?

Remember to ask yourself, *"What am I doing here? Is this for me? Am I getting what I need or am I adapting to what is offered? Am I repeatedly being told that what I am waiting for will happen later? Do I have the sense, at each moment, that this is a beneficial process for me?"*

You must take responsibility for the whole process. Otherwise, if you give away your responsibility, then, who is the healing for?

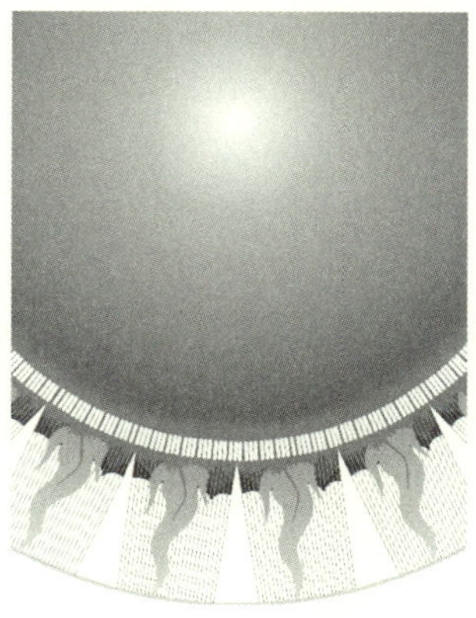

Resources

To help you in the process of becoming centered, and to sustain your effort, I have included some suggestions and resources. Consider what I have written a short introduction and a personal invitation for you to experiment further.

Getting rid of what does not support you

Many people forget that the key and goal of transformation is to let go of what holds you back. Often what holds you back is referred to as 'garbage.' Transformation is not about making a better home for your garbage. Spending long sessions talking about garbage, analyzing garbage, sharing garbage or seeking support for holding on to garbage, simply adds to the garbage. The biggest trap when seeking support for getting rid of garbage is to try to share and be accepted for the weight and importance of your garbage. Sometimes, it is a rude and disappointing shock that people do not want your garbage when it is offered. More often than not, those that do accept your garbage, have their own to share in exchange.

Remember what you came to do. The easiest and most direct way of dealing with garbage is to throw it out. Really. What holds you back is not your heart talking, it is the garbage.

Unfortunately the garbage i.e., your emotions, want to talk and share, and so talking about them may not be the best choice of action. Remember that emotions are like feelings without will. Being caught in expressing emotions, sharing them, analyzing them and so forth, does little good, unless the will is re-introduced. Therefore, as a starting place, use your will — and throw out all of the garbage!

What follows are various means of self-support for this process.

Exercise

Take a walk. Let your body move. If you are not already doing so, consider activities that can burn off or release tension. Examples of this are sports, running, yoga, aerobics, hiking, swimming, etc. Physical activity has the ability to release past issues and helps you to avoid being caught up with negative thoughts. You may think that you do not have time but, once a program of physical activity is initiated, there is usually more energy and the ability to do more with the time you have; the body benefits. Physical exercise not only releases tensions and helps in the release of garbage, but it also increases the level of oxygen, endorphins and supportive hormones that promote the feeling of well-being. You feel more grounded, more powerful and enthusiastic.

There may be initial resistance to exercise. Take this opportunity to reintroduce the will, and to strengthen it. As you strengthen your will, it becomes easier to release the issues that hold you back and prevent more emotional garbage from piling up. It is my experience that people who resist choosing exercise as a means, are holding on tightly to their garbage and need to have a good look at why they are doing this.

Walking

Walking is a very easy choice of exercise. If you are walking to help lose some weight, or to keep it down, be aware that to using walking in this manner requires a vital and lengthy walk. A walk that lasts for less than twenty minutes usually does little for losing weight, although it may help to maintain your weight level.

Walking is an excellent way to release tensions, worries and negative thought patterns. Walking helps to pull people out of their thinking and out of their head, by being more in touch with the body through movement and contact with the earth. Often taking a walk can get people past an argument or an impasse. Simply taking a walk, moving and getting out into the sun and fresh air, can help shift the state or situation that got trapped in words and concepts. We forget that to change things, action is required, even if that action is as simple as walking.

Hatha yoga

Hatha yoga is an ancient, powerful means to acquire mastery and true knowledge of your mind/body system and your life. This psycho-physical yoga is also a tried-and-true way of releasing tension and resistance, and a practical way of strengthening and centering the body. This physical aspect of yoga brings awareness to the body, and improves the health of both the body and the mind. Part of its success lies in its ability to release, over time, the impressions and emotions that we accumulate in the body, through specific postures. Although the poses may appear static, they are internally dynamic. We learn to focus on our energy, breath and awareness. Ultimately, and in stages, we learn to be centered in our life and, in the midst of everything that may come our way.

Even though yoga itself can be very beneficial, some practical discrimination is recommended. Choose a group or class that you trust, that feels good to your heart. Make sure that the instructor is well trained in anatomy and focuses on preventing injury. Also, be aware that for the most part, hatha yoga does not belong to any group or sect, so separate this from other offerings. Ask yourself why you are there. Don't get caught into becoming something someone else wants or needs. Also, avoid paying into the future. Pay for individual sessions, until you feel a particular group or instructor is good for you. Be mindful of how your body is changing and feeling. Is this working out for you? Are the instructors and helpers careful with the needs and range of movement of your body? Within the first few sessions if you are not deriving obvious benefit, consider other places or teachers.

Contemplation

The ability to stop for a moment and reconnect to your heart is a powerful and useful approach to freeing yourself of the past and moving closer to your own uniqueness and power. Contemplation is easy to learn and to do. It doesn't require a specific physical posture, but often, sitting comfortably in a way that keeps the spine straight, is a good way to begin.

If you would like to learn to contemplate, consider this starting place. Become aware of where you are, what you are feeling, physically. How does your body feel? How does the body balance itself against gravity? Observe your breath. Be aware of the breath moving in, resting, and then moving out again. Be aware of your thoughts. Do not do anything with them, just observe them; like driftwood on a river, or clouds in the sky.

You can select one thought or idea, and just hold it the way you would hold something in your hand. Do not run with the thought, simply hold it present in your mind and see where it leads you. In a way, contemplation is much like daydreaming, except that instead of feeling as if you are out there or absorbed in thoughts, you are absorbed in being and just observing your thoughts.

Contemplation – Going farther

The secret of contemplation is that you are allowing your mind to rest in your heart. The heart is actually the natural resting place for the mind. The head is not where the mind is supposed to be. When it goes there, it is often because of a disconnection with your feelings, with your heart.

The heart is a place of spontaneity, freedom and courage. Although we may take many 'things to heart,' and we have expressions such as 'heartache' and 'broken heart,' they actually are not referring to the heart, but to emotions and experiences that may keep you from experiencing your heart. It is important to understand that your heart contains within itself the ability to bring you to the present moment, to your joy and to the fullness of the experience in each moment. It is through re-connection to your heart that you are brought back to your true nature, to your love and joy.

In order to re-connect to your heart, in order to have your mind and awareness return to its true home in your heart, you have to stop 'trying' to do this.

The heart is already free and the mind already seeks that freedom and spontaneity. Stop 'trying' to take over what is a natural process. Let yourself be. Acknowledge your heart. Acknowledge your mind. Breathe. Allow the spontaneity of the moment lead you. Contemplation will teach you contemplation, if you let it. It is a great teacher. Sit back, relax and let the process happen, of itself. You will know when your mind rests in your heart. Some of the clues will be less thinking and more awareness, less of the old habits of thinking and more new and creative awareness.

Meditation

Meditation is very similar to contemplation, especially at the beginning. The main difference is that contemplation maintains awareness of what is happening around you while centered in the heart, while meditation goes a bit farther as an inward process. In a sense, contemplation surrenders the mind to the heart, and meditation further surrenders the mind and heart to the inner experience, the inner light or Self within. Like contemplation, meditation is neither difficult in itself, nor is it actually unfamiliar to most people. It is essentially a spontaneous process of revealing one's core. It can also be an experience in outward action, in the experience of being in the moment and of allowing yourself to flow in the moment. Artists and musicians who experience the profound connection and richness that occurs when they are in the 'zone' or when they 'let go,' can at times be very much in a state of meditation.

If you would like to try to sit for mediation, begin by sitting with your back comfortably straight. It is not necessary to cross your legs, but you are most welcome to do this if it is comfortable for you. If you are sitting on a chair, place your feet on the ground, and find a position that allows you to maintain the natural curvature of your spine. For most people this can be achieved by sitting at the edge of the chair, or by placing a small cushion behind the waist. You may want to put your hands on your thighs, palms down, with your index finger and thumb touching, forming a circle. This will help maintain the energy of your meditation within. Alternatively, you can rest your hands on your thighs, below your stomach, right hand folded over the left, palms up.

Relax. Use your breath to help you relax and unwind. Keep your back straight but not rigid. Imagine that the top of your head is being pulled up by a string. Feel the spine lengthening.

Stay alert, aware and focused. Meditation is not about taking a nap. Meditation is a state of subtle awareness. Become aware of the effect of gravity on your body, feel yourself anchored to the earth in the places that make contact with the ground or seat. Allow your body to relax so that you can focus on your inner process.

Become aware of your breath. Become aware of how the air enters you and how it leaves, and the sound it makes. Become aware of the rhythm of the breath; the in-breath, the out-breath and the times when the breath is balanced or still. As you breathe, let the thoughts just pass by. Simply observe your mind as you breathe in, as you breathe out and as your breath stills for a moment between inhalations and exhalations.

Let the cycle of the breath happen of itself, naturally, unforced. Allow the mind to simply observe. Consider treating each breath like the surf hitting the beach – each wave cresting as it hits the sand until the water reaches as far as it can go, partly settling into the sand and yet about to recede. For a moment, it lingers there. Next, the water begins to recede, until it reaches its lower level. For a moment, it lingers there, waiting for the next wave to come in, and then the cycle repeats itself.

As you sit, over time, the experience of meditation may become more subtle and dreamlike. Resist falling asleep. Instead become focused, steadfast and determined. Meditation is not just about going inside. It is also about becoming more aware and one-pointed.

At times, your thoughts may seem to be more active than you might expect, but do not let that concern you. In reality, for most people starting out in meditation, there is a shift from a cloud of many thoughts to fewer thoughts, where individual thoughts begin to stand out. It is just part of the process. Keep paying attention to the breath. Resist the temptation to do anything. Allow your mind to settle in your heart. Allow your self to be. Do not try to force your meditation or limit your experiences by your expectations.

At times, you may think that nothing happened, because it did not happen with your mind. Know that you are not your mind, that you are greater than just your mind and your thoughts about yourself. At some point, you may begin to drift off into meditation. If you drift, let that happen, don't try to control the process, even if it is to say to yourself *"Hey, I'm meditating!"* Acknowledge what is happening, but try to keep your mind and your need to control out of the process, or they will interfere and want to take over. Decide if you are sitting for meditation or whether you are sitting to have your mind do a song and dance about meditation. One of the consequences of a meditation practice is that the mind begins to focus on what you came to achieve; it becomes a tool for experiencing and revealing your core being.

Coming out of meditation, allow yourself to come out of your posture gently. If you felt that you did not experience meditation, don't worry. Each experience of meditation is different. Sometimes you can go inward deeply, at other times it can feel very shallow. Ultimately, meditation is a process of going within with awareness, and to do so effectively means that you have to let go of your expectations. It is not a controlled process that you can push yourself towards. It is more like welcoming a state that begins to cover you like a blanket. Meditation is the beginning of a journey of self-discovery, on the inside.

If you would like to pursue meditation further, look for a community of meditators. It often happens that when you are ready, what you need is revealed to you. Read over the section on seeking advice, because it may keep you out of trouble. Always test each group and its teachers with respect to what you need and why you are there. Test whether they are the embodiment of what they teach. It is important to choose a group which is aligned with teachers that have made great progress, otherwise, it will waste your time. Be prepared from the onset to change groups until you are satisfied with the results for your self and for what you came to receive. If in doubt, trust your heart and your gut feelings more than your 'head.'

Eating right for your body

What you eat affects your state. The wrong food can delay your progress and affect your vitality and energy level.

It is important to point out that before you make any significant change in your diet, you should first consult your health care provider to determine if there are any physiological conditions present that need to be taken care of first or that may have a bearing on your diet. Some people have hormonal imbalances or other conditions that need to be considered first.

Assuming that your health issues have been appropriately addressed, you may want to investigate several diets that have proven themselves to be effective, both in the short run, and as a lifestyle in the long run, without significant negative side effects. I personally recommend the *Zone Diet*,[5] as it was devised with attention paid to the real fluctuations that occur in people's physiology. The key components of this diet are that the proportions of carbohydrates taken in are kept closer to the amounts of protein. Among other things, eating too much carbohydrate is often responsible for the 'tiredness' people experience after a meal. In addition, a minimal amount of beneficial oil, or combination of fat and oil is maintained in this diet to keep the body out of choosing to go into starvation mode. This type of balance in a diet will serve and maintain you in the long run, without giving up too much of what you may have learned to enjoy. Quite a few popular diets have failed miserably by not taking these simple steps.

Light

One factor that tends to affect people and their energy level is the amount of light in their lives. We all tend to enjoy the bright sun of summer. Some of us tend to experience lower energy when the light level decreases towards that of a cloudy day or dusk. You may want to pay attention to this and add more light in places where you work or need to be more productive. People often make the mistake of trying to save money or energy with light, when it has such a profound effect on their state. The savings are often much greater in other areas.

You may also want to consider the kind of light you experience. Typically fluorescent light is uneven, with most of the illumination focused in strong peaks in specific parts of the spectrum. Some people can experience this as a strain. Some people also find that the 60 cycles per second pulse of fluorescent lighting, although barely perceptible, is stressful. Under these circumstances, it may be helpful to add an incandescent light to help even out the spectrum and harshness of the lighting. You might also consider trying full spectrum light bulbs, that more closely mimic the light outdoors.

Do not overlook the effect of light in your life. Take a daily walk to experience the full light of day.

Water

Did you know that most people, most of the time, are actually dehydrated? Did you know that you function best if you have enough water? For most people of average weight and build, daily water intake is suggested to be one eight ounce glass of water for each twenty pounds or so of total body weight. Water is necessary not only to replenish the body and to clear the body of toxins, but also to clear the body of emotional garbage. Whenever you are clearing through issues, processing, shifting or even recovering from a shock, water helps. This is partly why people are asked to drink water after a therapeutic massage.

Showers and baths

A shower or bath is a powerful tool to clear emotional garbage. If you are going through transformational process, clearing or reorganizing, or just coming home from a hard day at work, watch your state shift towards the better after a shower. It is almost as if the shower clears away the accumulated material of the day around your body. Your body's field is refreshed. If you are carrying concerns or hurts, take a shower and notice the improvement. During difficult times, I recommend at least two showers a day.

If you prefer baths, consider adding sea salt and baking soda in equal amounts, to the bath water. This combination has been used to clean the energetic field through the ages.

Sleep

It may seem a little out of place to talk about sleep, but many people ignore the value of sleep. Often, when there is a lot to do, the quality or amount of sleep may suffer. However, not getting enough sleep can make you less efficient in many ways, and often the result is counter-productive. Sleep is very important, especially when undergoing transformation or shift. Sleep helps in the process of integration and recovery. It even helps in normalizing or maintaining a healthy weight, partly because when we get adequate sleep, we tend to be more active during the day, and burn off more calories than when we are tired.

If sleep becomes difficult to achieve, consider not eating an hour or two before you go to sleep. Drink water or herbal tea. If thoughts are keeping you awake, consider writing them down in a journal (do not take too long) and then take a shower to help clear your energy before going back to sleep. Condition your body to prepare for sleep by going to sleep at the same time each night. Decrease the amount of light in the room, as light interferes with the body's production of melatonin that supports sleep. Alcohol also interferes with melatonin production. You may find it helps you to move active electrical or electronic devices a few feet away from your body, especially from your head. Your orientation to the earth's magnetic field may also have a bearing on your sleep. Experiment with the direction that you choose to sleep in.

A journal

For some people, a journal can be a place to begin the journey of taking care of themselves, of taking responsibility for their lives. At the end of the day, writing in a journal is a great way to evaluate what you did, what happened to you and what you learned. Journaling is an opportunity to re-visit your lessons and contemplate changes in yourself or your choices. Most people going though personal shifts have some difficulty with continuity. We often repeat the same mistakes and miss the same opportunities because we do not keep a consistent review of our efforts and opportunities. For people who have a tendency to act one way in one situation and another way with other people or situations, a journal or diary allows an opportunity for integration across all of these parts of ourselves.

Another useful application of a journal is closure, as in it we can write what we wished we had done or said, or what remains to be done or said, so that we don't have to carry it with us. It is always best to just let go of things that hold you back. If that is not possible, it is far better to write it down in a notebook than to carry it in your muscles and bones.

A journal can also be a place to acknowledge our successes. Do not forget to write down the positive things that have happened to you. Your diary is a dialogue with yourself. If your diary becomes a place of negative thoughts, that aught to let you know that you are really just dumping on yourself! This is not the purpose of a diary or journal! It is an instrument for moving forward and towards your greatness.

Consider writing in the diary, then taking a shower. You may find your sleep more restful.

A journal – going farther

It is not necessary to write too much, or to recount all of the details of what happened. It is important to jot down where you need to make changes and improvements. Where you feel these improvements can be made, write down some practical suggestions. At the left of each suggestion, draw a little check box. The next time you return to the journal, see if you have applied any of your suggestions. If you have, you can start checking them off. Go back to previous entries and see if there are other suggestions that you made for yourself. Did you act on any of these? If you tend to forget, consider listing these on a piece of paper and looking at them at the beginning of the day. Consider getting a very small notebook just for suggestions, so that you can check your progress.

When you do move forward, acknowledge your effort. Check off the item in your list and consider adding a comment with respect to your experience of making the effort. You may want to reward yourself in other ways by doing something that is fun, or that you have been postponing. Each time you take care of yourself, the process tends to get easier, but do not slack off. Keep moving forward.

Spring cleaning for the soul

I once knew someone who made great efforts to clear away his accumulation of unneeded books and paperwork. He had literally accumulated box after box of material that held little benefit, yet he also had difficulty letting go of these things. His process of discarding was to make piles of all of this stuff, to sort it, organize it and determine what was what. Almost all of the energy went into sorting and very little into letting go. In the end, he had innumerable piles of stuff, without empty places to keep the order he was trying to achieve, and he had very little sorted material ready for disposal. Often, in a rush to prepare for company, the piles would be thrown back into the boxes, and at other times, the complete process would be repeated again.

What is missing in this picture? Does any of it seem familiar to you? We can get stuck clearing away old stuff when we organize it according to our past associations. The problem is that we often hold on to possibilities, avoidances, to past glories and past wounds. Each thing we hold on to stays because we avoid adding our will to it, dealing with it, and truly letting it go. Therefore, I suggest another alternate way of taking action with our accumulations.

Determine what is too valuable for you to throw away; documents, mementos and articles that are precious to you and that you can use in the future, or that may bring recollections that are positive or grounding in your life. These need to be put away carefully.

For the rest, you need to determine their usefulness to you. Were these items potentially useful for you in the past, or are you holding on to them because years ago you thought that they may be useful in the future? Now may be that future, so ask yourself if they remain useful. If you are not sure, consider picking them up and just allow yourself to sense if they add benefit to you. You can tell, just by feeling, if something is being kept because you sense you will need it, or it is being kept because in some way you are afraid or resistant to throw it away. If you sense resistance, ask yourself – does my energy go up or down as I hold this? If it pulls your energy down and is of little practical or financial value, then why are you keeping it?

If you are still stuck with some items, try this strategy: Calculate the actual amount of space these questionable items occupy in proportion to the rest of your space. Let us say they occupy half a room and there are five rooms, so they occupy ten percent of your space. What is ten percent of two years of your rent or mortgage? That is how much money you are investing in keeping them for the next two years. For many people, this means you are investing about two thousand dollars in keeping this stuff. Is it worth that much? Would not ten percent more free space be a better investment? Remember that just keeping stuff that has little or negative value is not only tying up space that you are paying for, but also your time and energy. How much time and energy do you think you are going to spend going over and over this stuff? Are there not activities that are more productive?

Therefore, evaluate what needs to be kept and what needs to be disposed of on the basis of real value. Often what we hold on to, holds our fears. I have known teachers that have kept all of their books, manuals and associated material for all of the courses that they ever taught. This also included course software and technology that has long since come and gone. All of this material was kept as a crutch, because the teachers were afraid that they did not know enough to teach the course on their own. Somehow, keeping all of this material made them feel safer, but as a result, they never developed trust in themselves. The piles of books held their fear and lack of trust in themselves.

I have also observed some people holding on to clothes and wardrobes that they have not worn in years and are not likely to. Of course, something inside them senses that they don't look good in these clothes anymore, but they are kept anyway, just in case, out of fear of letting them go.

We can also be that way with furniture. I remember a living room that was dominated by an L-shaped couch. No matter where that couch went, in whatever orientation, it killed the energy of the room, and divided up a large room into little spaces. The couch was not thrown out, because it was such a great bargain! In reality, it occupied and dominated over a fifth of the residence, and in real money, using the calculation strategy introduced earlier, cost twice as much to keep each month, as the actual price paid for it, bargain not withstanding. Finally, getting rid of it cleared so much space and energy, that it was not missed.

I am not advocating that you go out and throw things away, just for the sake of it. Instead, determine what is of value to you.

less of the signs. Are you likely to achieve what you want? Do not disregard the signs; that is one of the most common mistakes that people make. They notice something is not working for them and they continue anyway. Perhaps your solution lies elsewhere, on a different path. Find out.

A passing thought

We seek in others what we hold back in ourselves! Often, when we receive what we seek from others, we have difficulty accepting it in until we open up to ourselves. Therefore, to bypass all of the frustration, start with giving yourself what you need. It is then more likely for what you seek to manifest for you and you will be able to appreciate it and others will appreciate you.

You need to love yourself. You need to love yourself now, not when you lose ten pounds, not when you finally meet someone, not when you do a good job, get a degree or retire. You need to love yourself now, as you are, with all of your foibles and warts and false beliefs about yourself.

It is only at the moment when you love yourself that you can escape what you were never meant to be. Once you love yourself, you will take care of yourself. You will make the effort to make the changes that bring you closer to your heart and to living in joy. You will not wait. You will not postpone joy and trust. You will stop buying into the game that if you are good you can love yourself. You will break out of the delusion that if you do what others want of you, then you can love yourself.

The truth is, that it takes courage to love yourself. **You have that courage.**

It takes great humility to be willing to accept the freedom and greatness that lies within your own heart. **You have that humility and that great heart.**

It takes responsibility to honor yourself and to take care of your feelings. **You are responsible and able to honor.** You have the ability to respond appropriately to take care of your feelings and your best interests. You have proved it by taking care of others. Now, you need to demonstrate this to yourself so that your trust can grow. You need to demonstrate this to the part of you that has always held the power to open the door to the light, to joy and to delight in your life.

When that part of you gains your trust, you will shine your own love and joy. Your courage to shine will help others to begin trusting themselves. **You will be centered and you will be positively and irrevocably contagious.**

Love yourself now. This is true freedom. Be positively contagious. All else is delusion.

> *Every moment of your life is infinitely creative and the universe is endlessly bountiful. Just put forth a clear enough request, and everything your heart desires must come to you.*
>
> Gandhi

Appendices

Appendix 1: Feelings, Emotions and States

A Summary

The Relationship of Feelings, Emotions and States

The experience of our core

Most of us, at one time or another, have had a deep experience of ecstasy or bliss, a sense of profound awe that defies description. Do you remember such a time? Perhaps a beautiful sunset filled you with awe and stopped your mind for a second or two; a most delicious desert caught you by surprise; a disarmingly welcome smile melted your heart, and for a moment, time stood still for you. Often, the spark comes unexpectedly within our everyday experience. These are moments when we connect to our true being, our core, our own spirit or essence.

The experience of our feelings

More often, we experience these feelings when we are directly connected to our heart. These can be feelings of love, joy or a sense of aliveness and openness to being present, to being in the moment and in the flow of life. These feelings arise spontaneously whenever we reconnect to our hearts as the joy you feel when you meet a good friend, as the richness of life you experience when you are in love, or when you are doing something that you truly enjoy.

Feelings of separation

When something happens that disrupts that connection with our hearts, we experience feelings of separation, such as, fear, anger, sadness or hurt. These feelings reveal our loss of connection and urge us to do something about it. For example, when someone interrupts you, insults you or invades your space without asking, anger may be your way of responding immediately. Through anger you fix it, try to make it better and let the other person know how you are feeling. That anger is trying to reconnect you to your own heart so that you can feel joy again.

Emotions

When anger fails to reconnect you, it turns into an emotion. Emotions occur when things get stuck. In fact, one way of looking at emotions is that they are our experiences of being stuck outside of our hearts. Emotions hold our separation from our heart, our wounds and our hurts, and, they seek to express our relationship with that separation and hurt. They differ from feelings which express our relationship with our hearts.

This is why we over-react to circumstances with emotions such as fear, envy or rage. At those times, our wound is talking. Unfortunately we cannot heal from this place; we can only add to our sense of being hurt. It is only when we calm down or become re-connected to our hearts that healing can take place.

Emotional states

What happens when you start to accumulate emotions? They begin to drain your energy, and over time, if you let them, they begin to define who you are. Imagine that every emotion that you absorb is like a rock that you put in a knapsack. After a while, the weight of the rocks becomes a burden and dragging the heavy knapsack behind you takes energy, effort and time. To a greater and greater extent, you are being defined by the accumulated weight of that knapsack. It may seem absurd to have to drag it everywhere you go, but this is exactly what people do with their emotions, and this is what their emotions do to them.

Just like that rock-filled knapsack, our accumulated emotions can become holding patterns - negative emotional states which define us: we begin to put ourselves down, expect negative things to happen, hold negative self images, and even harbor regret or bitterness.

Negative emotional states

These are negative states that people often confuse with feelings and emotions. They keep us separated from our heart, and to some degree, hold our willingness to stay separated. One of the key ways these states are different from feelings or emotions, is that our ego tends to embrace them as definitions of ourselves. Due to maintaining these self-images, others can manipulate us and push us to defend a false sense of who we are, through pride, resignation, rage or vengefulness.

Positive emotional states

There are also positive states which are separate from feelings and hold our separation from our heart. Our ego tends to embrace these states much like the negative states mentioned earlier. These positive emotional states are much more pleasant; like being admired, competent or nice. To a large extent we see them as qualities or states that are good to have. However, they define us in ways that limit the fullness of our experience. In identifying with these states, we seek to be what others want, or to be what is acceptable, rather than being free to be as we are. In this respect, they can be hooks just as much as the negative states mentioned already.

Look at the positive states as carrots, and the negative states as sticks to prod you on. When identifying with either of these types of states, you become vulnerable to being manipulated by others.

Behind our willingness is our hope to be healed of the underlying emotions and separations from our heart. However, most people, by seeking healing on the outside and making others responsible, only get more and more entangled, instead of being freed.

I have summed up the relationship of feelings, emotions and states in the table below.

The relationship of feelings, emotions and states:

Primary States	Experience of deep connection at our core. *Examples: Ecstasy, Universal Love*
Feelings of connection	Experience of being connected to our hearts *Examples: Joy, love*
Feelings of separation	Experience of immediate disconnection from our hearts *Examples: Fear, anger*
Emotions	Past experiences of disconnection from our hearts *Examples: Hurt, blame*
Positive emotional states	States that hold separation from our hearts, but have a positive association and may support our reconnection to our hearts. Our false identification with these states may also maintain our separation from our hearts. There is a level of judgment and of being defined by others. *Examples: Deserving, vindicated, respected*
Negative emotional states	States that hold separation from our hearts and have a negative association. Our false identification with these states may block our reconnecting to our hearts. There is a level of judgment and of being defined by others. *Examples: Despair, unloved, defiant, outraged*

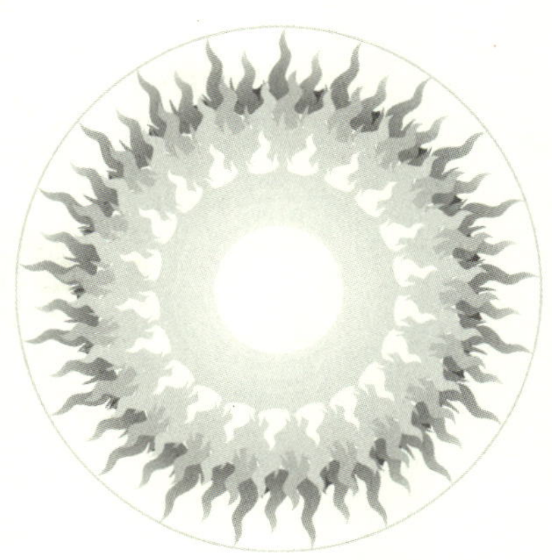

Appendix 2: Feelings, Emotions and States

A Listing

This is an addendum for the chapter 'Feelings and Emotions.' Here you will find lists of primary states, feelings, emotions, positive states and negative states. The purpose of the lists is to help you distinguish between these categories in order to get a better sense of what they are, and what they can mean in your life. Be aware that some words have more than one meaning, and that people tend to interchange some of the meanings. For these reasons, some words may appear in more than one list. This is not a definitive list, but is designed as a guide.

Primary States

I am calling Primary States those which are deep, inner connections to the core and to the Self. Primary states are associated with being in the heart, centered and fully in the moment, and in deep connection to spirit and our inner divinity.

State of compassion
State of ecstasy
State of pure joy
State of unit
State of universal love

Feelings of Connection

These positive feelings are associated with being in the heart, or connecting to the heart.

alive	delight	happy	open
amazed	ecstasy	joy	vibrant
awe	enthusiam	joyful	warm
compassion	glad	love	

Feelings of Disconnection

The following negative feelings are associated with being pulled or tugged from the heart, or away from optimal being. It is specifically these feelings which we must paid attention to, in order not to lose the connection to our heart.

Please note that 'fear' is not only a feeling of separation from the heart, but can also be an emotion, when we are holding that separation. As a response to separation, the feeling of anger is the expression of our will seeking reconnection. We experience anger as an emotion, when it holds our disconnection and disowned will.

afraid	bored	pain	sorrow
alarmed	fear	sad	tired
angry	grief	scared	wounded
bad	hurt	sick	

Emotions

Often, people will define themselves by saying "*I feel . . .* ," or "*I am . . .* ," using words from the following list. However, rather than these being direct feelings that connect us to the heart, they are emotions holding our separation from the heart. Emotions are reactive.

They seek re-connection, yet this is possible only through re-introduction of the will and through performing actions that break through the experience of separation from our heart or core.

aversion
awkward
baffled
bashful
belligerent
bewildered
blame
boredom
bothered
bugged
burned up
caustic
chagrined
challenged
closed
concerned
confused
contemptuous
craving
cross
cutoff
defensive
dejected
dependent
desperate
despondency
disappointed
discontented
disdainful
disjointed
dismal
dismayed
dispiritedness
dissatisfied
distorted
distracted
distressed
disturbed
dreadful
drugged
edgy
embarrassed
enmity
enraged
envy
exhausted
fatigued
fighting mad
forlorn
frightened
frustrated
furious
greedy
grumpy
horrified
hostile
hyperactive
impatient
infuriated
inhibited
intense
irked
irritated
jealous
lethargic
listless
mad
miffed
miserable
mixed-up
moody
needy
nervous
overwhelmed
painful
panicky
pissed-off
scared
seething
self-conscious
shaky
shocked
shy
sullen
teed off
tense
ticked off
timid
torn
trapped
troubled
unsure
upset
uptight
violent
worried
zealous

Positive Emotional States

Often, people will define themselves by saying "*I feel . . . ,*" *or* "*I am . . . ,*" using the words in the following list. However, rather than these being direct feelings that connect immediately to the heart, or being emotions that express your separation from the heart, they are states that can maintain your separation from the heart. Most of the words imply judgment, or are definitions imposed by others.

Without question, some of these states are good to be in, but for the purpose of this book, they are on this list because they can also keep you from reconnecting to the heart.

These states limit your openness to a more narrow area of experience, or they define you as separated from the heart, either directly or subtly. For example, you may experience yourself worthy, or maintain a self image of being nice, even at the price of your integrity to your heart and feelings.

accepted
admired
adored
adventurous
affirmed
alert
amazed
amused
appealing
appreciated
approved
ardor
assertive
at-ease
attractive
balanced
benevolent
brave
brilliant
capable
cared for
cheerful
comfortable
comforted
competent
concerned
confident
congruent
connected
consoled
content
courageous
creative
curious
daring
delighted
deserving
desired
determined
eager
elated
embraced
empathetic
enchanted
esteemed
exacting
excited
fond
forgiven
free
friendly
generous
genuine
gifted
good
gratified
hopeful
idolized
important
in control
indrawn
independent
infatuated
intelligent
interested
justified
keen
liberated
light
liked
lovable
loyal
lustful
nice
not troubled
optimistic
passionate
patient
peaceful
perfect
pleased
pleasured
popular
powerful
precious
proud
protective
pure
purposeful
rambunctious-
rarefied
reassured
regarded
relaxed
relieved
respected
responsive
revered
rewarded
secure
seductive
sensual
sincere
smart
strong
superior
supported
sure

sweet
sympathetic
tender
tolerant
tolerated
tranquil
triumphant
trusted
turned on
unblemished
uncomplaining
undemandin-
gunderstood
unique
untroubled
useful
valiant
valuable
vibrant
vindicated-
wanted
wide awake
worthy
yearning
youthful

Negative Emotional States

Often, people will define themselves by saying "*I feel . . .*," or "*I am . . .*," using the words in the following list. However, rather than being direct feelings that connect immediately to the heart, or emotions that express your separation from your heart, these are states which maintain your separation from the heart. As with the previous list of positive states, most of these words imply judgment. They differ from positive states in that they continue to separate you even further from your heart. They hold an ongoing negative definition or judgment as to who you are, and to some degree, they are acceptances of that very separation and judgment.

abandoned
abhorred
abused
abusive
accursed
aggressive
alone
annoyance
antagonistic
apathetic
arrogance
attacked
averted
bashful
beatenbe-
trayed
bitterness
blamed
blemished
bored
castrated
cheated
complacent
compromised
confusion
consumed
contaminated
contemptuous
controlled
cruel
crushed
cynical
dead
deceived
defeated
defective
defiant
degraded
dejection
dependent
deplorable
depressed
despair
despised
destroyed-
destructive
detested
devastated
dirty
disappointed
disconsolate
discontented
disdainful
disgusted
disillusioned
dissatisfied

distant
dominated
domineering
drained
dread
dreadful
drowning
dumb
dying
egotistic
empty
endangered
enmity
envious
estranged
evasive
exasperated
exhausted
exploited
explosive
exposed
failed
failure
fat
fatigued
fearful
fed-up
flawed
floundering
fooled
forgotten
forlorn
fouled
friendless
frustrated
futile
galled
gloominess
guilt
guilty
hated
hatred
heavy
helpless
hopelessness
humiliatedg-
loomy
hypocritical
immobilized
impotent
inadequate
incensed
inconsistent
incompetent
indecisivein-
dignant
ineffectual
inferior
inferiority
inimical
injured
insecure
intimidated
intolerance
irrational
irritated
isolated
judged
judgmental
justified
lethargic
like a loser
limited
loathed
lonely
lost
manipulated
marked
masked
masochistic
melancholic
misery
misinformed
misunderstood-
mixed-up
naked
needy
negativity
neglected
obligated
offended
out of control
outraged
overlooked
oversexed
oversized
panic
paranoid
perplexed
persecuted
perturbed
pessimistic
phony
pitiful
pity
possessed
possessive
powerless
preoccupied
pressured
private
protective
proud
provoked
punished
putdown
putoutpuzzled
rage
regret
regretful
rejected
reluctant
resentful
resigned
responsible
restrained
revengeful
rigid
rigidity
sadistic
scapegoated
secretive
selfish
sensitive
shame
shamed
shocked
shy
sinful
smothered
soiled
sorry
sorrowful
spiteful
stressed
stubborn
stupid
subservient

suffering
suspicious
tempted
terrified
threatened
torn
trapped
torn up
traumatized
turned off
ugly
unable
unacceptable
unaccepting
unappreciated
unbalanced
uncertain
uncomfortable
undermined
undervalued
undisciplined
unfortunate
unfulfilled
unimportant
unintelligent
unlikable
unloved
unlucky
unresponsive
unpopular
unprepared
unsupported
unsupportive
usurped
unsure
unwilling
unworthiness
used
useless
vain
vengeful
violated
vicious
victim-ness
vindictive
vulnerable
weak
weary
withdrawn
worn-out
worried
worthless

Appendix 3: Forming Layers

The layers of personality and identification

In the chapter, *How Did We Lose Our Inner Child?* we looked at how experiences of being unaccepted can lead us to abandon our relationship with our feelings and our heart, and, how we forsake our selves in order to experience love and acceptance on the outside from our parents, and later, from our peers and society in general. This chapter looks at the process of forming layers from a more graphic perspective. Here, we will review, how the layers of personality, which eventually hide our inner child from others and from ourselves, are formed.

The first layer: The beginning

Let us go back a little bit to where all of this started, beginning with our birth. When we are born, our sense of time changes. We are thrust into an experience of time that moves forward, while being very much in the moment.

The process of being totally centered in our core and learning to outwardly project our experience to the world around us, is being illustrated as an expansion from our center.

Our natural process is to act authentically, outwards from our core, as we feel and flow in the moment.

Early in our lives, we become aware of the importance of the people we bond to and reach out towards. We are often drawn out of ourselves, and sometimes away from our core, in the process of interacting with our parents and others who are significant in our lives. I am illustrating this tendency as the adapting layer we form which then extends in the direction of our parents.

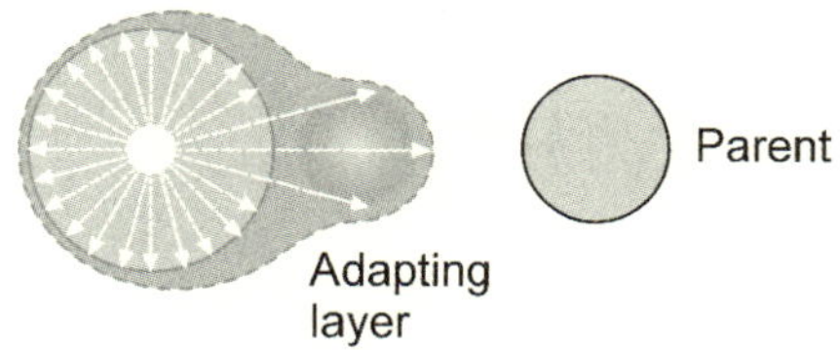

Those that become significant to us can pull on our experience of being centered.

If we learn to focus and identify with that part of us which adapts to what our parents want or demand, we risk believing this adaptation as who we are. Our parents may also reinforce our mistaken identity by interacting with our adapted behavior and personality, and ignoring us as we truly are.

As a consequence, we begin the process of ignoring and then losing our connection to our core, how we truly feel, and what

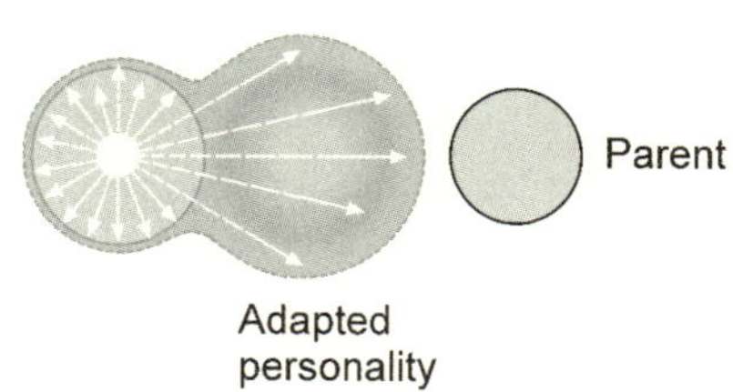

As we identify with the adapted part we begin to lose connection to our core.

we truly need and want. At the same time, we begin to focus on being accepted from the stance of our adaptation, and a layer is formed around our core. It is from this layer that we tend to continue interacting with others.

If we don't get encouraged for being ourselves, we may then hold the sense of being unacceptable or unworthy in this early layer of adapting - the layer that seeks being taken care of and being loved at home and by our family.

Wounds of this type reveal themselves later when people go into a rage, often over something that was rather trivial. They may go into a tantrum, because when they were two years old they were not allowed to express or test their power. Now, perhaps at middle age, after too many drinks or in a confrontation with others, they are triggered back to a wound in which they sense their power had being ignored.

The second layer: Learning about polarity

The world that children enter into is polarized: there is the polarity of home versus the outside world; the polarity of mother and father; the polarity of male and female. A balance between polarities is important. Therefore, it is important for the parents to get along with each other and to demonstrate their love and affection for each other in front of the child. In this way, the child feels supported in extending their reach beyond the polarity of home and the larger world outside, in part, because the child has already witnessed polarities affirming each other. If the child feels accepted and supported by her parents, she is more likely to stay centered and strong as she leaves the safety of the home and reaches out into the world.

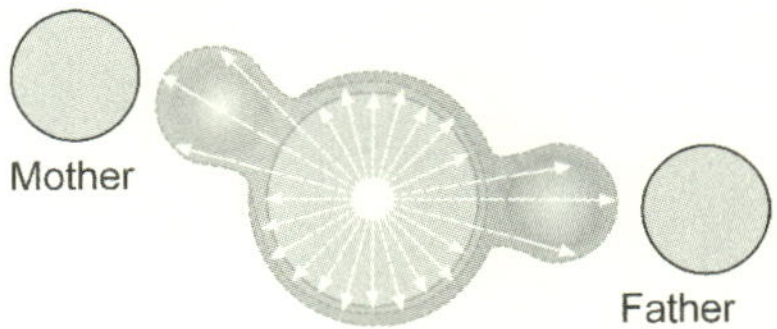

The next layers of personality form by our adapting to the experience of our individual parents, both mother and father.

Often, when people hold a wound in that early layer of adapting to their parents, they later experience difficulty being around children that are at the same age as they were when they experienced their hurt and wounding. Some people react by being overly strict with children of that age, or experience children as a nuisance as a result. Some get confused and do not know how to hold their power with children who push the buttons which reveal wounds they hold in that layer of their personality.

I remember being at a party at a couple's home where their very precocious and free spirited three year old wandered around socializing with the guests. At this party were top executives and people from various professions who wielded considerable power and influence in their careers. The little girl would enter into dialogue with these executives, who were at first amused by the advance of this child. However, their state changed as the child asked them what they did for a living, followed by whether they liked their job, why they don't, and then, why they don't do something about it? This was more than disarming. Innocently, she was addressing the little boy or girl inside each of these executives. And, to the degree that their own disconnection to that young place within them was revealed, they felt powerless and did not know what to say or do. These powerful executives could only shrug their shoulders and wait for the little girl to pick on somebody else!

Some people hold severe wounds in these places of adapting. Some hold frustration, anger or rage. Because the wound is held in a young layer of adapting, it expresses itself in childish or immature behavior when it is triggered. Often, the emotional charge takes over, and later it is denied.

If the rage came from experiences of abuse, the denial can support a pattern of abuse that continues through several generations. That denial comes from the parent not taking responsibility for what they did and for their own healing. That denial also becomes part of the wound for the child.

To the degree to which children feel supported in being centered, they are able to feel loved, honored and cared for. To the degree in which they have experienced being pulled out of their center and have held onto wounds and negative experiences, they have difficulty feeling loved, loving themselves, honoring themselves and taking care of their feelings and best interests.

By the time the child is about six, their peers begin to take on an added importance in their development. It is with their stance of how lovable or worthy they are and their sense of power and importance, that children enter into interactions with their peers

The third layer: Our relationship with our peer group

A great deal of literature has been written about the effect of the family on a child's development. There is considerable debate as to whether children develop their personalities regardless of their parenting, or whether early family life and interaction with parents moulds the emerging personality of the child. This is the 'nurture versus nature' controversy. At the time of this writing, the evidence strongly supports the genetic predisposition of the child as the stronger factor. It would appear that the parents function is to draw out and support the child's potential. However, traditionally ignored in this controversy is the effect of the peer group on the child.[6]

If you watch children, you will notice how aware they are of children their own age. They play with other children and learn to interact with each other. By the time they go to school, their acceptance by other children becomes very important to them. Needing to be accepted, appreciated and welcomed by their peers pulls many children out of their core, in much the same way that the process happened with their parents and family. However, now the children are older, and their interaction with their peer groups begins a process of pulling the children away from their parents, or begins diminishing the effect that parents have on the unfolding of the child. This is a normal, if not a desired part of disconnecting from family patterns and beginning to develop patterns closer to their own sense of independence. Yet, sometimes, this new layer compounds and confuses an already

off-centered situation

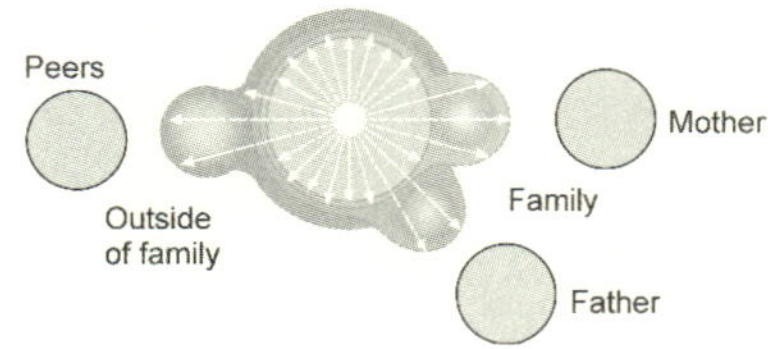

The peer group becomes an important molding factor as children get older.

By the time the children are twelve or so, the peer group begins to have more power and sway in the child's development than the parents do. By that time, children have developed the capability of being one personality and set of behaviors at home with the parents, and another personality and set of behaviors with their peers.

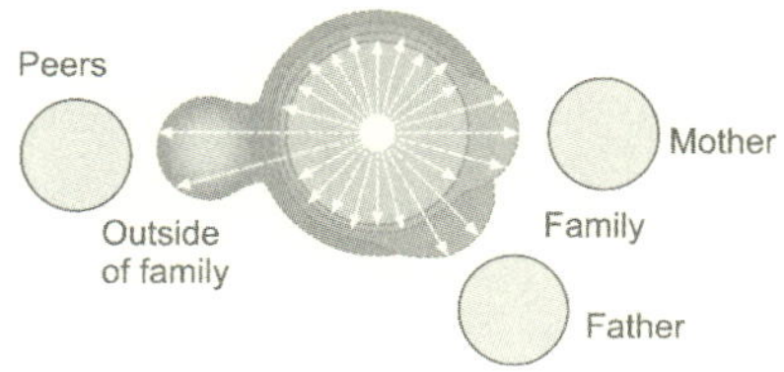

Over time, children become more identified with fitting into their peer groups than with their immediate families

The significance of the peer group, and peer group pressure, can be seen in how children at this age begin to shift their whole orientation within themselves and to the world. That shift is away from noticing and validating the world from the perspective of their individual experience, and towards an experience of the world from a more collective point of view. It is not only a shift in value and focus towards the peer group, but also a shift to the culture through the eyes of the peer group. In a way, the world unfolds as a big game, and learning the 'game' and being good at it becomes more than just a matter of pride. This is the age when children even feel they know better than their parents!

These shifts in identification are dramatically illustrated

by looking at children's drawings. If you compare these with drawings made by adults, you may be surprised to find that they are indistinguishable after about the age of twelve or so.[7] After that age, children and adults draw less what they see or feel, and more what they believe and what their culture believes; the only exception is the drawings of artists.

By the early teen years, the power of the peer group begins to overshadow that of the parents, becoming the primary engine for personality development. Around this time, most parents are surprised to discover that their children are not who they thought they were. The children adapt to the parents, speak their language and culture while at home. Outside the home, in the new larger world, they expand to become who they see themselves to be and how they are as defined by their peers.

By the time the children are twelve or so, they have formed several layers to their personality. The first layers adapt to their parents. The next layers adapt to their peers and to their place in the world.

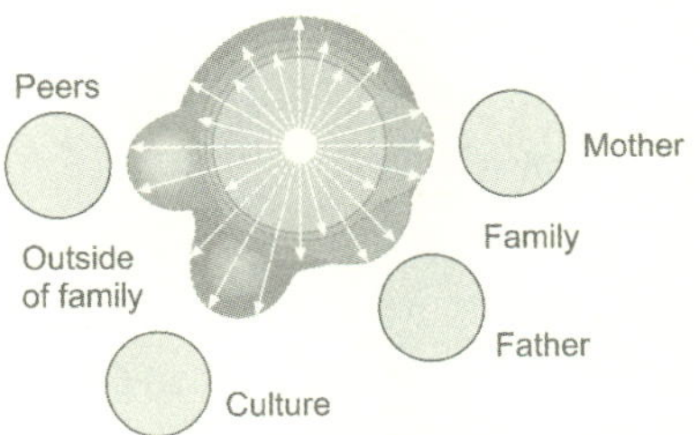

By the age of twelve, the identification with peers and culture becomes a primary focus for many children

Positive experiences with their peers strengthen the child's power and ability to be a player in the larger world. If the child, now a teen, also had positive experiences at home, then he is more likely to continue gaining confidence in the world while still acting from their heart and joy; he is more likely to go into life with courage and trust.

If there have been serious negative experiences in relating to their peers, or if negative experiences at home have held them back from participating with their friends, then the child may find himself more stuck in these layers of his personality. Experiences of not being centered or of being disconnected in relationship with their hearts may translate into escape, over-objectification, fear of success or a sense of not belonging. To protect these wounds, teens may be attracted to systems, beliefs and disciplines that deny feeling, communication or openness.

The degree to which teens can return to center, to their power and joy, depends in part to how trapped they become in these layers of adapting to their peers, as for some, being accepted by their peers can become as important as life itself. Although these layers extend their ability to function in the world and are necessary vehicles for mastery and effectiveness, they can also be over-identified with, if the connection to the core and heart has been lost.

The fourth layer: The intimate relationship

By adulthood, most people experience a relationship with someone that takes them out of themselves in a new and exciting way. Although there may have been other relationships already, a relationship can now form at a level that challenges the family as the primary relationship.

The age of majority, of adulthood, is rarely about being fully functioning as an independent and mature being, rather, it is more about the recognition that at this time, one is ready to leave the nest of the family home. Rarely can one do this, as more often, the home is replaced with something else. At this time, that something else is often an intimate relationship.

For many people, the first important close relationship outside of the parents, involves an attraction, an intensity, a longing and a closeness that makes life worth living. Life can become vivid, rich, alive, and full of love. What happens, outside of hormones, that propels this situation?

Part of the answer lies in the fact that this new relationship has the polarity and intensity to rival that with the parents. We can connect with another soul, to the level of spirit, to a deeper and more transformative level than we could have experienced with our parents. Part of that power comes from a re-connection to our core, at the level of intimacy, trust and bonding. For some of us, it is the first time that this level of intimacy and transformation has been accessed. This is a time of magic, of dreams and possibilities, as this is for some of us, the first time that we can connect to another person at the level of spirit, heart and timelessness.

What forms at this time is a 'third entity' beyond the two people. It is the relationship itself, created and supported by the fact that both people experience each other with their hearts. There may be a formal declaration of this new connection to the world and the parents, through marriage or by living together

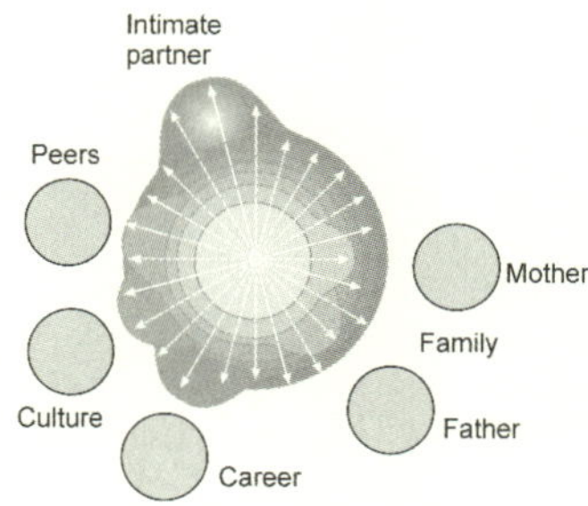

The pull of a deepening relationship with an intimate partner

This new bond and its declaration may also begin a period of conflict due to the pulls that previous relationships have already established. The parents may not approve, or may play games that prove that the young adult is still under their power. The friends may challenge the time and focus that they have lost and want back. The school or career demands may fly in the face of the changes happening.

Within the intimate relationship itself there may be challenges or conflicts. Some of these challenges may be that having established a close relationship, one or both of the partners begin to reveal the emotional charges and wounds that are still held in their earlier layers of development. These may be issues related to experiences with their own parents and early childhood, and later, with peers. In fact, some of the hooks and qualities that may have contributed to choosing this particular intimate relationship, may be the very same unfinished emotional business reaching for healing and consummation.

If the relationship can survive being a conduit of past issues, it can transform to a higher level of being. The sense of a relationship as a 'third entity' may be re-absorbed, so that there are only two people in tune with each other, connecting from their core, from their hearts, expressing feelings and joy.

The partners, at the same time that they lose themselves in each other, find themselves. The energy, love and attention that reaches out, is met and received with the same. This is being in love. One has allowed someone so deeply into one's heart, that separation when it occurs, is painful.

There are now four main layers to the personality, the inner child, the adapting to the parents, the adapting to the peers and, to varying degrees, the adapting to an intimate partner.

The new layers: the new family

When a couple has children, they are faced with new experiences, a re-connection to the timelessness and joy of an infant and a new challenge. That challenge is to maintain the intimacy the couple shares with each other, while being pulled by the new responsibility of their young child.

An infant is totally dependent, totally accepting and open. If the infant becomes the central relationship for either parent, the relationship of the couple may be in jeopardy. Sometimes, the mother becomes so absorbed with the child that the husband comes to feel as if he is number two or three in the pecking order. If this unfolds, he may feel isolated, especially if he begins to be treated as one of the 'kids' by 'super mom.' This can damage the polarity between husband and wife to such an extent as to kill the sexuality and enthusiasm between them. The experience may be likened to betrayal. Emotions and hurt may begin to separate the couple and become part of this new layer of interaction. Past issues may find a vent in this situation. The connection to the heart may be lost and replaced by blame.

The husband is often not innocent. If he is like most fathers that go to work while the mother stays with the young children, he may feel the added weight of keeping his job at all costs. Over time, he may find that the pull of work and associates have intensified to the point of challenging the time spent at home, with spouse and later the children. The husband may forget his connection to his heart and to his family, through adapting to work and to the acceptance of his peers, co-workers and friends. He may even redefine his marriage from the point of view of his friends and co-workers, and he too may come to blame his spouse for his lot in life.

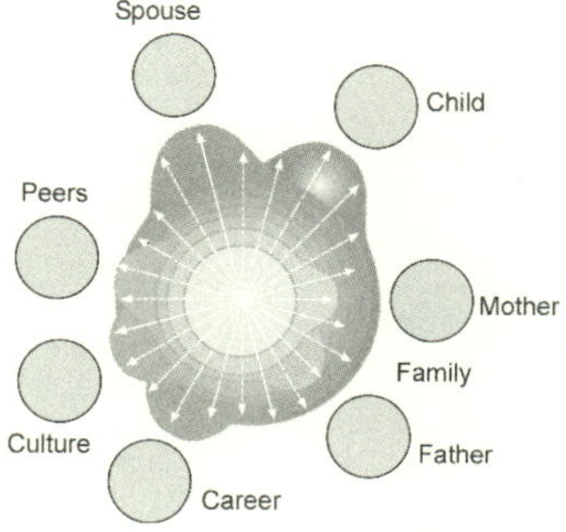

A new child and family refocuses the identification of the couple

It is very important that the couple weathers these challenges and remains their own primary focus. Children need the sense of stability, display of affection and healthy sensuality that comes from parents who are committed to each other as the most important relationship in their lives. The couple's relationship must come first, before career and even before the children, and the children need to know and adjust to this. Only in this way, when the children themselves grow up, will they feel comfortable with affection, honesty and protecting what they value.

The consequence of layers

It is very important to understand, that all the formed layers can be an unfolding in the way we manifest joy and power in the world. If we stay centered, owning our power, then these extensions into life are part of our growth, part of our expansion and joyful mastery of the world around us.

These layers can also be an enfolding. If one or more of the layers hold negative experiences, if we identify too much with an extension of ourselves that over adapts to the needs of others, then here, is where we lose energy and power. It is from that layer that we are pulled away from our own center, and are kept off balance in our relationship with other people.

Glossary

This is a short glossary of the terms that I am using in this book. These are not the decisive definitions for each term. What I have endeavored to do, is provide you with a working idea of what these terms mean in relation to the concepts expressed in this book.

Addiction
An addiction is a situation where you have entered into a dependent relationship with something outside of your self. In some way, it brought relief, or a heightened sense of joy, at the beginning. Now, it negatively affects your life and you experience difficulty in letting go of this dependency.

Advice
Advice comes from the Latin word *advisum*, meaning 'opinion'. Advice originally meant an opinion from someone not directly involved, or from someone acting at a distance. (We must always bear in mind that advice is often given by people that do not walk in our shoes, so to speak. Advice must always be tested, to see if it is beneficial for you.)

Authentic Self
Our authentic self is the part of ourselves that is primary, primal and not defined by others or by outside influences. (See self.)

Being Centered
Being centered is our natural state. We are centered when we are directly connected to our core and reside in the freedom, spontaneity and courage of our hearts. In that stance, we resist being pulled away from our heart or feelings by events on the outside.

Being in the Moment
Being in the moment is the experience of being fully present in what you are doing, feeling and experiencing. It is similar to what

people refer to as being 'in the zone,' but the experience can also be deeper and more profound. Being in the moment means that you are not being handicapped by the past or the future, by expectations, unrealistic fears, judgments, by what others think or by your own projections.

This can be the state of someone fully absorbed in what they are doing, such as, the experience of a musician, dancer or martial artist who are in flow. We encounter this state more often in the child-like spontaneity of someone who trusts and feels that they are loved, accepted and supported in being who they are

Blame

Blame is similar to a grudge, in that we make someone else responsible for our emotional charge and disconnection from our heart. We assign blame to others when we deny our responsibility for our feelings and will, and make them the active agency. In so doing, we put ourselves in a reactive frame of reference; we make others responsible for our own disconnection to our heart and we expect them to make the actions and changes that we deem necessary for us to be willing to reconnect to our heart.

Chakras

The chakras are dynamic, subtle energy centers that support the energetics of the body-mind system. Most literature refers to seven main chakras supporting and energetically linked to the base of the spine, the lower abdomen, the solar plexus, the heart, the throat, the place between the eyebrows and the area above the top of the head.

Core

In this writing, the core refers to our true essence and our integrity. When we are in our core, we are in the state of being centered and aligned with our authenticity and integrity.

De-centering Event

An experience that pulls us out of relationship with our core or center. We experience this separation in our heart and feelings. When we can not reconnect to our core through our hearts, this event can take the form of injury, fear and separation from the heart.

Ego

The ego is the part of us that learns to anticipate and takes care of us in the world. It acts as an interface between our essential or authentic self and what we consider the world to be. In many ways, the ego acts like our programming. We have the capacity to 'weed' out the 'programming' we may have accumulated in our ego that does not benefit us, our authenticity, so that our ego remains healthy.

Emotions

The residue of our feelings divested of our will or responsibility. We hold on to emotions in order to maintain the possibility of healing them and thus reconnecting with our heart. (See feelings)

Energetics

The term 'energetics' relates to our personal energy and how that energy manifests. This includes our thought process, perceptions, the way we move, the way we hold issues, our feelings, sense of power, and as well as subtle, spiritual and psycho-physical dynamics. The term also includes the way we store impressions in our mind and body. If this definition seems too encompassing, know that we are energy beings, and as such, many of our problems arise from blocks to the optimal flow of our energy.

Faith

Faith is a willingness to trust in something greater or outside of what we can grasp or test in the moment. The sacrifice of faith is in our willingness to let go of our limitations and ways which make ourselves small and closed to receiving what the universe has to offer. 'Blind faith' involves giving away our will as opposed to 'true faith' which involves willingness.

Fear

Fear, as a feeling, is the experience of disconnection or separation from our hearts, as may occur from an emotional shock, trauma or contracting experience. As an emotion, fear is the experience of holding on to the contraction. In that respect, fear is a non-coherent resonance that holds the experience of being separated from the heart, core or self.

Feelings
Our feelings are the immediate perception and experience of our energetics, as felt in our hearts or in relationship to our hearts, before being edited, delayed or re-interpreted by our expectations, thoughts and avoidances. (See emotions)

Future
The future is the place where we project and hold our expectations, hopes and fears not yet resolved in the present moment.

Grace
Grace is the power to open ourselves to what the universe has to offer, and to our own divine nature. There are two variants of this word, one capitalized, one not. The word 'grace' refers to our own openness to receiving, whereas 'Grace' refers to the transformative and expansive power offered to us through a higher power.

Heart
The term heart used in this book refers to the energetic or subtle place in us where feeling, spontaneity and courage arise.

Hooks
A 'hook' is a pit-fall. We experience 'hooks' when our own unprocessed, unresolved or denied issues are still attached to being healed by others, or by something outside of ourselves. Hooks come from emotions driven by need and reactiveness.

Inner Child
In this writing, the inner child refers to the spontaneous and feeling part of our nature which plays and feels in the present moment, and relates directly with that part of us that experienced joy as a young child.

Joy
The spontaneous experience of being alive in the present moment, being in our power and in a state of flow. Joy is also the feeling of being connected in our hearts.

Luck
Luck is a greater than normally expected positive outcome. Often we associate luck with faith, expansion and openness. For example, beginner's luck involves openness as a result of less expectation. Our willingness to be more expansive brings more opportunities for luck to manifest. Our faith in the future, opens us to possibilities that may still come our way.

Mind
That part of ourselves that tries to own, hold, respond, grasp, understand and react to our experience of being. In meditation, we can go beyond the mind to realize that we are much more than the limitations that our mind places on our awareness of being.

Past
Although we may take the past, present and future as a given, we really only live in the present. Our past is where we hold memories, challenging experiences, emotional issues and wounds that still seek healing in the present moment. Our past can also hold the limitation, disassociation or contraction we place on ourselves.

Power
Personal power is our ability or capacity to transform or make a true difference within ourselves and in the world around us by being connected to our core or heart. The experience of the flow of our power, or true nature, is joy.

Present
The only time in which we actually feel, experience, heal, and exist is the present. The past and future can be considered as dissociations created out of the present. We talk of someone being 'present' as an indication of how much they are in the present moment, and

not distracted by their past or future issues.

Re-Centering
Re-centering is the ability to return to our core, to our heart and place of well-being.

Responsibility
The ability to own our feelings and choices, whether these choices take us towards connection and integrity, or disconnection and loss of center. Although we may assign responsibility to others, and even blame them, the ultimate responsibility for our life rests with us and our chosen responses.

Self
The self is our center, our core, a place of no attachments. Often, there are two variants of this word, one capitalized, one not. The 'self' refers to our center of being, beyond ego. The 'Self' refers to the deepest essence of our being, from where our light, awareness and consciousness manifest.

Shadow
Shadow is the term used for the held back, repressed or denied parts of ourselves which darken our experience and perception of the present moment. The shadow relates to those parts of us that we often deny. It is dark, in part because of the energy and light we lose in the process of pushing these parts of us away, and in part because what we deny within ourselves, we manifest through making others responsible for holding or embodying.

Shift
What is referred to as shift is a process of change that occurs in our energetics; a change in the way we hold our issues and in the place that we act from. A shift is different from simply having a change of belief or understanding. A shift usually involves the release of inhibiting issues and attachments.

Sin
The material that has been identified with and has clustered around the heart, keeping you away from being in joy, being connected to your heart and in the present moment. Sin is also what keeps you from connecting to your core and to the Self.

Trust
Trust is a willingness to accept ourselves as we are, our process, or the people or processes around us. When we speak of 'trusting ourselves' we are supporting and aligning ourselves with our own coherence and integrity. Trust is different from faith, in that with trust we maintain, acknowledge or express our will fully as we are, while with faith, there is a willingness to be something different or new, usually by letting go of something that blocks our way.

Will
Will is the power of continuity between heart and action. Will seeks to maintain integrity, wholeness and our freedom to act. As a result, we assert our will in order to maintain our integrity as we step into the next moment or into the future. Our will hides in our anger, as we act to regain our connection to our heart.

Bibliography

1. Bob Dylan, *Gotta Serve Somebody* (Slow Train Coming, Copyright © 1979 Special Rider Music).

2. Stanley Milgram, *Behavioral Study of Obedience. (Journal of Abnormal and Social Psychology* 67, 371-378, 1967).

3. Lucia Capacchione, *The Power of Your Other Hand* (North Hollywood, California: Newcastle Publishing Co., Inc., 1988).

4. Thomas S. Kuhn, *The Structure of Scientific Revolutions* (Chicago: University of Chicago Press, 1962).

5. Barry Sears, *The Zone* (New York: HarperCollins, 1995).

6. Judith Rich Harris, *The Nurture Assumption: Why Children Turn Out the Way They Do* (New York: Simon & Shuster, 1998).

7. Betty Edwards, *Drawing on the Right Side of the Brain* (Los Angeles: Jeremy P. Tarcher, Inc., 1989).

Index